The OLYMPIC EXPERIENCE in Your School

(Grades K–3)

10 9 8 7 6 5 4 3 2 1

ISBN   1-58000-117-3

TCM   3749

DIRECTOR OF OPERATIONS . . . . Robin L. Howland
PROJECT MANAGER . . . . Bryan K. Howland
AUTHOR. . . . . Sarah Kartchner Clark, M.A.
EDITOR. . . . . Eric Migliaccio
COVER ARTIST . . . . Brenda DiAntonis
ILLUSTRATOR . . . . Bruce Hedges
IMAGING . . . . Rosa C. See

Published in association with
and distributed by:

Griffin Publishing Group

18022 Cowan, Suite 202
Irvine, CA 92614
www.griffinpublishing.com

Teacher Created Materials, Inc.

6421 Industry Way
Westminster, CA 92683
www.teachercreated.com

Manufactured in the United States of America

Table of Contents

Introduction

Dear Educator,

You and your students are about to embark on an exciting exploration of the Olympic Games! Every two years, the world stage opens to the excitement and competition of the Olympic Games. The Olympic spirit permeates the countries of the world and the hearts of the spectators and the athletes. The goal of this book is to capture this spirit and to assist in creating the Olympic experience in your school or classroom.

At the beginning of this unit of study, your students will receive the title of "Junior Olympic Scouts." As Junior Olympic Scouts they will be ready to explore the Olympic Games firsthand. Your students will learn the history of the Olympic Games and how they are organized. Students will experience teamwork, goal-setting, and hard work. Students will learn of Olympic athletes and their contributions to the story of the Olympics Games. Students will be inspired with past Olympic stories and memories. Finally, the sights and sounds of the Olympic Games will be brought to life with your very own Olympic experience. Junior Olympic Scouts will be involved in the planning, decorating, competing, and reporting of the Olympic Games, and the awarding of the Olympic medals.

This study of the Olympic Games is organized by venues. Each venue contains lessons and activities that span the curriculum and expose students to required skills. Junior Olympic Scouts will work through each Olympic venue. The Olympic venues in this book are as follows:

———————— ☆ **Venue 1: The Olympic History and Traditions**

———————— ☆ **Venue 2: The Olympic Spirit Throughout the World**

———————— ☆ **Venue 3: The Olympic Athlete and Olympic Sports**

———————— ☆ **Venue 4: The Olympic Experience in Your School**

As Junior Olympic Scouts complete the tasks and lessons of each venue, they receive a sticker to put on their Olympic passport. They will need a completed passport in order to compete in your school or classroom Olympic Games. The experience in each venue will prepare Junior Olympic Scouts to compete in the Olympic Games.

This study of the Olympic Games will take approximately one month. Each venue will take one week to finish. The culminating week will be the school or classroom Olympic Games. This week should include preparation, as well as the competition aspects of the Olympic Games. Use this book to organize and provide the framework for your own Olympic Games. Feel free to adjust and modify the activities to fit the needs of your students and your school.

The Olympic Experience: An Overview

Here are some suggestions you can use to organize this unit in your classroom. Feel free to alter these suggestions and ideas to meet the needs of your students and your school.

Setting Up the Unit

Begin the preparation of this unit by reading through the venues and the activities. Familiarize yourself with the goals and expectations of this unit. First, read the Olympic Skills and Objectives on pages 6–7 and determine which objectives and skills will be met with this unit. Next, determine the bulletin board or boards that you will be using in this unit and get the materials ready. Create a "word wall" in your classroom to post the Olympic vocabulary words from page 12. This will make these words easily accessible for student writing and brainstorming. Make copies of pages you will need for each week of this unit. Be sure to start off with the Olympic Scout badges and the Olympic Passports on pages 9 and 10. Then, you are ready to begin!

Olympic Scouts

Each student will be given the title of "Junior Olympic Scout" at the beginning of the unit. The goal of a Junior Olympic Scout is to look for information about the Olympic Games. The scouts will complete tasks and assignments in preparation for the Olympic Games. Each Olympic Scout is given a badge to decorate and wear (page 9) and a blank Olympic passport (page 10). As students travel through the Olympic venues, they are given stickers (page 11) to place on their Olympic passport. Students will need a completed Olympic passport to compete in the Games.

What Is an Olympic Venue?

This unit is divided into sections entitled "venues." Each venue focuses on a different topic related to the Olympic Games. It will take approximately a week to complete the activities and lessons in each venue. At the conclusion of each venue study, students will collect a sticker to place on their Olympic passport. This provides an easy way to keep track of assignments and projects your students have completed. The culminating activity and the last venue will be the participation in the classroom- or school-wide Olympic Games. Read the brief description of each Olympic venue.

☆ Venue 1: The Olympic History and Traditions

At this venue, students will be learning the history of the Olympic Games and the traditions associated with them. Where was the first Olympic Games held? What do the rings on the Olympic flag symbolize? Why were only men and boys allowed to compete in the first Olympic Games? What is the Olympic torch? What happens at Opening and Closing Ceremonies? All of these questions and more will be answered as students work through this venue. Students will be making their own torches, medals, and other Olympic art and decorations.

The Olympic Experience: An Overview *(cont.)*

☆ Venue 2: The Olympic Spirit Throughout the World

Which countries compete in the Olympic Games? What makes each of these countries unique? As students work through this unit, they are assigned a country to research. Students will learn the customs and traditions of their assigned countries. Students will also learn of the roles these countries have played in the Olympic Games. Has the asssigned country been an Olympic host? Students will make flags of their countries and put together a museum display of artifacts and information about the countries they have studied. Students will study how their countries integrate with the rest of the world, and delegates will be invited to participate in a cultural summit to discuss international topics.

☆ Venue 3: The Olympic Athlete and Olympic Sports

At this venue, students will take a closer view of the Olympic athlete. What are the requirements to compete in the Olympic Games? What makes an Olympic athlete great? What skills does an athlete utilize in his or her quest for an Olympic medal? What inner strength is needed? Students will be given an opportunity to examine their own goals and their own lives in a quest for something greater. Student will also learn about the types of sports in which athletes compete. What is the history of these sports? How is a sport admitted as a competitive sport in the Olympic Games?

☆ Venue 4: The Olympic Experience in Your School

With the wealth of information the students will have gained about the Olympic Games, they will be ready to participate in an Olympic sport of their own. At this venue, students will be assigned to a committee. Each committee will be given a specific assignment to play at the Olympic Games in your school. The committees are the following:

➤ *Decorating and Advertising Committee*
➤ *Documenting and Reporting Committee*
➤ *Ceremony Committee*
➤ *Judging and Recording Committee*
➤ *Celebration and Awards Committee*

More information on these committees can be found on pages 84–85. Each committee group will also be competing together as a team in the Olympic Games. Students will use teamwork in order to win as many medals as they can.

Parent Volunteers

When you are ready to have students compete against each other in the Olympic events, you will want to have parent volunteers on hand to make this run smoothly. You may choose to have a parent meeting to explain the working of the Olympic Games so that each parent is informed of the role he or she is to play. Try to keep your Olympic Games as organized as possible so that it will be enjoyable for all. For more information on how to organize your own Olympic Games, turn to Venue #4.

Olympic Skills and Objectives

The opportunities for student growth abound in this unit on the Olympic Games. Each subject of the curriculum will be addressed. Here is a list of objectives and skills addressed in this unit:

Art

The students will do the following:

- know the various purposes for creating works of art
- create art through a variety of mediums and materials
- know how people's experiences can influence the development of artworks.

Language Arts

The students will do the following:

- read for understanding
- establish purpose for reading
- use context clues to determine meaning
- uses story maps and webs
- discuss ideas with peers
- brainstorm and take notes
- use strategies to draft and revise written work
- use strategies to edit and publish written work
- include a beginning, middle, and end in writing
- write a letter including the date, address, greeting, and closing
- write a narrative about a personal experience
- write a biographical sketch of an Olympic athlete
- write a persuasive composition on the Olympic Games
- write a poem about the spirit of the Olympic Games.

Life Skills

The students will do the following:

- identify the qualities and characteristics of great Olympic athletes
- identify strategies to foster the positive and supportive characteristics of Olympic athletes
- contribute to the overall effort of a group
- use conflict-resolution techniques
- use interpersonal communication skills
- set and manage goals.

Olympic Skills and Objectives *(cont.)*

Math

The students will do the following:

- use a variety of strategies to solve word problems
- add and subtract numbers with decimals
- understand the basic measures of length, width, height, and weight
- organize and display simple bar or line graphs
- understand the difference between the U.S. Customary and Metric measurement systems.

Physical Education

The students will do the following:

- use a variety of basic locomotor movements (e.g., running, jumping, galloping, hopping, skipping)
- engage in basic activities that develop cardio-respiratory endurance
- use a variety of basic object-control skills
- participate in activities that provide personal challenge.

Science

The students will do the following:

- know that the position and motion of an object can be changed by pushing or pulling
- know that friction will slow the speed of an object
- determine the difference between water (liquid), ice (solid), and vapor (gas).

Social Studies

The students will do the following:

- compare and contrast the modern and ancient Olympic Games
- consider how people use ideas from the past to enrich the present
- complete a map of ancient Greece, identifying key locations in the story of the ancient Olympic Games
- analyze the contributions of ancient Greek society in helping to establish the foundations of the ancient Olympic Games
- create suggestions for promoting the spirit of peace in their homes, schools, and communities
- comprehend that each country has customs that are understood and accepted by its people
- study familiar and unfamiliar customs of other nations
- prepare a museum display to help tourists visiting a foreign country
- understand how politics and nationalism have influenced the Olympic Games
- become aware of the lives of children in other countries
- compare and contrast events happening in the world with those happening at home.

Olympic Bulletin Board Ideas

There are many bulletin board ideas that you can use to bring the Olympic Games into the classroom. Read the following ideas and select the ones that interest you most:

1. If the Olympic Games are taking place at the same time that you are teaching this unit, cut pictures and newspaper articles from the newspaper to place on the bulletin board. You can have students complete a Who, What, Where, When, Why, and How outline on what is happening in the news. Post pictures of Olympic athletes and see if students can match the pictures with the names.

2. Make copies of the Olympic pictograms on page 56–60. You can have students write brief reports on each Olympic sport, which they can then post under the corresponding pictogram on the bulletin board.

3. Create a word wall bulletin board by collecting and writing words from or related to the Olympic Games. Students can use this word wall as a reference in their own writing projects and assignments.

4. Have students draw pictures of people competing in their favorite Olympic sport. Students can write imaginary journal entries about their day at the Olympic Games. Post the journal entries next to the illustrations.

5. Make copies of the pictograms on pages 56–60. Cut apart the pictures and glue each to a 6" (15 cm) square of red, green, blue, or yellow construction paper. Cover the bulletin board with white paper. Print the words "The Olympic Games" in large letters across the top center of the bulletin board. Add the labels "Winter" or "Summer" on either side of the board under the Olympic heading. Attach the pictograms under the correct heading (either "Winter" or "Summer").

6. Make a copy of a world map or attach a world map to the bulletin board. As countries compete in the Olympic Games and medals are awarded to the countries, keep a record of the number each country has received. Attach yarn from each country to an index card. Record the medal count for each country on the index card. Change the medal count daily or as the need arises. Use the map to discuss distance, continents, geography, time zones, and the Olympic Games.

7. Read the information on the Ancient Olympic Games on pages 15–17. Discuss these Olympic Games with your students. How are these Olympic Games similar or different from the Modern Olympic Games? Have students draw a picture taken from the history of the Olympic Games. Post these pictures in correct order on the bulletin board.

Olympic Scout Badge

Teacher Note: Make a copy of this badge for each student to wear. Allow each student to color and decorate his or her badge.

Olympic Passport

Teacher Note: Give each student a piece of 11" x 14" construction paper. Fold the paper in half. On the cover, glue the picture with the words "Olympic Passport" on the front (see below). Glue a passport chart page on the inside of the folded construction paper. (This page should be a piece of paper with four large, blank, rectangular boxes on it. These boxes should be the same size as the venue stickers on page 11.) When students have finished the assignments and work for a particular venue, they can cut out that venue's sticker and place it on their passports. Venue stickers are found on page 11.

Olympic Venue Stickers

Color the sticker from the completed venue. Cut it out and glue it under the correct venue on your passport.

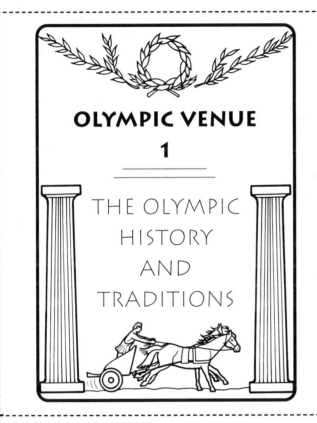

Olympic Vocabulary

Create a word wall with these words posted so that students can refer to them in their writing and reading. Review a few words each day so that students have time to become familiar with them. Based on the abilities of your students, you may choose to use words from each of the three groups.

Simple Words

run	play	boat	row	ball	ride	team
world	ski	swim	snow	sled	ice	win

Basic Words

bronze medal: a round, decorative piece of bronze (metal) given to the third-place winner(s) in each Olympic event

event: a contest in a sports program

Olympic flame: the fire that burns in the cauldron at the Olympic Games as a symbol of peace between the competing nations

flag: pieces of material sewn together and decorated with symbols to represent a country or a group of people

gold medal: a round, decorative piece of gold given to the first-place winner(s) in each Olympic event

Olympic rings: five colored, interconnected rings that symbolize peace among the continents of the world

silver medal: a round, decorative piece of silver given to the second-place winner(s) in each Olympic event

sport: a physical activity engaged in for pleasure rather than out of necessity

Advanced Words

amateur: an unpaid athlete who competes without monetary compensation

ancient: very old or from long ago

athlete: a person trained in games requiring physical skill, endurance, and strength

closing ceremony: the program that ends and closes the Olympic Games

compete: to try to win a prize or reward

Greece: the Mediterranean country where the Ancient and Modern Olympic Games were first held

IOC: International Olympic Committee

Olympic Games: a series of international athletic contests held in a different country every two years. There are winter and summer Olympic Games.

Olympic pin: decorative brooch worn to symbolize events and experiences of the Olympic Games

opening ceremony: the program that begins and opens the Olympic Games

modern: relating to the present time or time not long past

professional: a paid athlete who makes a living competing in sports

qualify: to show the ability and skills needed to be on a team or to participate in a contest

stade: the length of the Olympic stadium during the ancient Olympic Games in Greece

USOC: the United States Olympic Committee, which organizes the Olympic Games and the Olympic Team in the United States

Olympic Trivia

A quick and easy way to share Olympic information is with Olympic trivia. Each day, write one of the following questions on the board. As students enter the classroom, they will read the question and record their answer. Students can work as teams to determine the answer. Remind them it is not about being right or wrong, but making a guess and learning. Reveal the answer later in the day to give students a chance to think about the question. Answers can be found in the answer key on page 95. You can also write trivia questions of your own or encourage your students to submit trivia questions to be answered.

☆ Ancient Olympics

1. Who participated in the Ancient Olympic Games?

2. In what year did the Ancient Olympic Games begin?

3. What did winners in the Ancient Olympic Games receive?

4. What did the ancient judges wear?

☆ Modern Olympics

5. When were women first allowed to compete in the Olympic Games?

6. Which country's team is the first to walk in the Opening Ceremonies?

7. What do the doves at the Olympic Games represent?

8. What is used to light the Olympic flame?

9. What is the prize for second place at the Olympic Games?

10. How many years are there between the Summer and Winter Games?

11. In which country did the Modern Olympic Games begin?

12. What do the five rings stand for?

13. Which Olympic Games has more events, summer or winter?

14. What country held the first Olympic Winter Games?

15. What is one of the words in the Olympic motto?

16. What does the winner of each event receive?

OLYMPIC VENUE

1

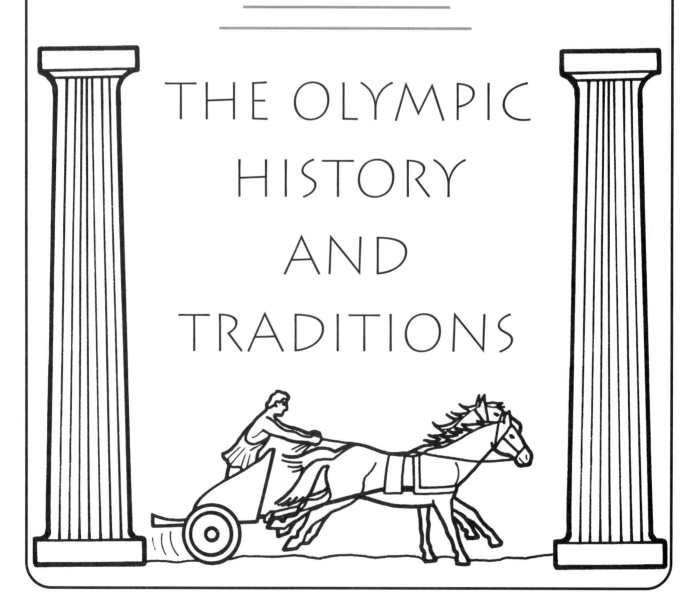

THE OLYMPIC
HISTORY
AND
TRADITIONS

Ancient Olympic Games Mini-Book Directions

Materials: copies of pages 15–17 for each student, construction paper (black, yellow, blue, red, or green), stapler and staples, scissors, crayons or markers

Directions:

1. Distribute copies of pages 15–17 for students and have them cut the pages apart. Provide construction covers. You will need to cut the construction paper to the right size.

2. Have the children assemble the pages of the book. Check the page order before stapling the cover on the mini-books.

3. Distribute crayons or markers. Instruct students to follow your directions before using any of the crayons or markers.

4. Read each page of the mini-book one at a time. When you have finished reading, allow time for students to color the picture. Discuss the meaning of any difficult words with students. Repeat this process until you have completed all the pages.

5. Practice choral reading the mini-book at least three times. You can also have students read independently, with a buddy, or with an adult volunteer.

The Ancient Olympic Games   1

Ancient Olympic Games Mini-Book

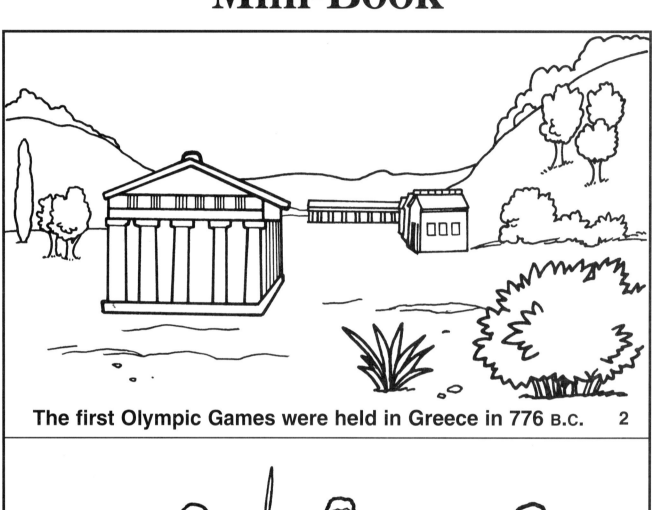

The first Olympic Games were held in Greece in 776 B.C. 2

Only men and boys were allowed to compete. 3

Ancient Olympic Games Mini-Book *(cont.)*

There was a foot race called a "stade."   4

There was also a chariot race.
Winners won a crown of olive leaves.   5

Ancient Olympic Games: Show What You Know

In the box below, draw a picture of what you think the ancient Olympic Games must have been like.

Comprehension Check

1. Where did the ancient Olympic Games begin? _____

_____

2. When were the first Olympic Games? _____

_____

3. Who played in the ancient Olympic Games? _____

_____

4. Name two ancient Olympic events. _____

_____

5. What did the winners get for a prize? _____

_____

For younger students: Answer three of the questions.

For older students: Answer all five questions. Then, on the back of this paper, write a question of your own for someone else to answer.

Modern Olympic Games Mini-Book Directions

Materials: copies of pages 19–21 for each students, construction paper (black, yellow, blue, red, or green), stapler and staples, scissors, crayons or markers

Directions:

1. Distribute copies of pages 19–21 for students and have them cut the pages apart. Provide construction covers. You will need to cut the construction paper to the right size.

2. Have the children assemble the pages of the book. Check the page order before stapling the cover on the mini-books.

3. Distribute crayons or markers. Instruct students to follow your directions before using any of the crayons or markers.

4. Read each page of the mini-book one at a time. When you have finished reading, allow time for students to color the picture. Discuss the meaning of any difficult words with students. Repeat this process until you have completed all the pages.

5. Practice choral reading the mini-book at least three times. You can also have students read independently, with a partner, or with an adult volunteer.

The Modern Olympic Games

1

Modern Olympic Games Mini-Book

First modern Olympic Games were held in Athens, Greece, in 1896. 2

Athletes from all over the world come to compete. 3

Modern Olympic Games
Mini-Book *(cont.)*

Women were finally allowed to compete in 1900. 4

Olympic athletes hope to win an Olympic medal. 5

Modern Olympic Games: Show What You Know

In the box below, draw a picture of something about the modern Olympics.

Comprehension Check

1. Where did the modern Olympic Games begin?_____

   _____

2. When were the modern Olympic Games started?_____

   _____

3. When did women begin competing in the Olympic Games? _____

   _____

4. Name three Olympic events. _____

   _____

5. What do the athletes that compete in the Olympic Games hope to receive?

   _____

For younger students: Answer three of the questions.

For older students: Answer all five questions, then write a question of your own for someone else to answer.

Map of Ancient Greece

This is a map of the mainland of ancient Greece. Can you label the cities on the map? The first letter of each city's name has been provided for you. Use the box below to help you. Now look up a map of Greece today. How does it compare with this map?

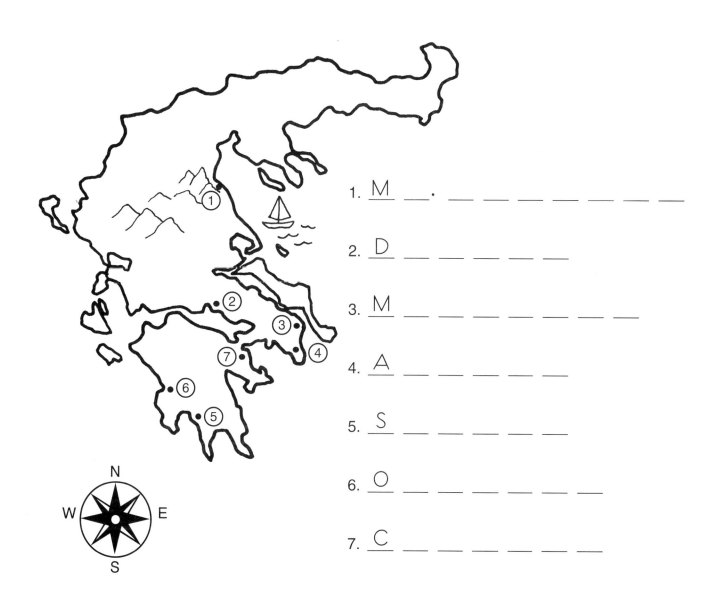

1. M __ . __ __ __ __ __ __ __ __ __

2. D __ __ __ __ __

3. M __ __ __ __ __ __ __ __

4. A __ __ __ __ __ __

5. S __ __ __ __ __ __

6. O __ __ __ __ __ __ __

7. C __ __ __ __ __ __ __

Olympic Sites and Cities

Corinth	Mt. Olympus
Olympia	Athens
Sparta	Marathon
Delphi	

Olympic Symbols and Traditions

The Olympic Games past and present are filled with symbols and traditions that have stood the test of time. Read about the following symbols and traditions of the Olympic Games.

The Olympic Motto

The Olympic motto is "Swifter, Higher, Stronger." Father Henri Didon, headmaster of the Aucueil School near Paris, France, wrote these words. The motto represents the athletic ideal of the Olympic Games.

The Olympic Creed

Baron Pierre de Coubertin, the founder of the Modern Olympic Games, wrote the Olympic creed in 1896. It reads:

The most important thing in the Olympic Games is not to win but to take part, just as the most important thing in life is not the triumph but the struggle. The essential thing is not to have conquered but to have fought well.

The Olympic Rings

Five interlocking rings represent the five major continents of the world. Their colors (in order from left to right) are blue, yellow, black, green, and red. These colors were used because at least one of them appears in the flag of every nation of the world. These colorful rings are used to symbolize friendship of all humankind.

The plain white background of the Olympic flag is to symbolize peace throughout the games. The colored rings are center in front of the white background. Though the colors of the rings hold no official significance, some believe each color of the rings represents a particular continent. They feel the black on the flag represents Africa, blue represents Europe, yellow represents Asia, green represents Australia, and red represents North and South America.

The Olympic Athlete's Oath

At the Opening Ceremonies, the athletes take an oath promising to compete fairly and to be good sports. Here is what they say:

We swear that we will take part in these Olympic Games in the true spirit of sportsmanship and that we will respect and abide by the rules which govern them, in the true spirit of sportsmanship, for the glory of the sport and the honor of our country (or teams).

Olympic Symbols and Traditions *(cont.)*

The Olympic Torch

The tradition of the modern Olympic torch began in 1936 at the Berlin Games. It was meant to represent a link between the ancient and the modern Olympic Games. It is still an important part of the Olympic Games today.

The torch is lit, as it was many years ago, by the sun at Olympia, Greece. The torch is then passed from runner to runner in a relay that travels from city to city across the world until it reaches the host city. Once the torch reaches the host city, the flame from the torch is used to light a flame in a cauldron at the Olympic Stadium during the Opening Ceremony. The flame burns continuously throughout the Games.

The Olympic Flame

The Olympic flame is lighted by the Olympic torch during the Opening Ceremonies of the Olympic Games. The Olympic flame is one of the most visible symbols of the modern games. The tradition of the flame originated in ancient Greece.

Olympism in Today's World

Olympism is a set of values that enhance the physical, intellectual, and spiritual growth of participants through sport, art, and music while promoting friendship and understanding in the world.

Olympism teaches athletes these things:

1. Work hard to be healthy and exercise. It's important to be involved in physical activities and to take care of our minds and bodies.

2. We should be good sports and have good sportsmanship. Athletes should treat each other with respect and dignity.

3. We can learn a lot from sharing our cultures with each other. There are many things of value in each culture and from each country.

Opening and Closing Ceremonies

Teacher Note: For younger students, read and discuss this page with your class. For older students, pair students with a partner to read and discuss it.

Opening Ceremonies

The Opening and Closing Ceremonies of the Olympic Games have always played a vital role in carrying out the Olympic feel and tone of the Games. The ceremonies are steeped in tradition dating back to the ancient Olympic Games.

In ancient Greece, the Olympic Games opened with the judges walking out in royal purple robes, a heralder, and a trumpeter entering the Hippodrome. The Hippodrome was the oval track used for the races. The judges took their places, and then the competitors paraded past them in chariots drawn by four prancing horses. The job of the heralder was to call out the name of each competitor, the name of his father, and his city. When this was finished, the Games were officially open.

The Opening Ceremonies ushered in the modern Olympic Games of 1896, nearly 2,500 years later. This time, 258 athletes from 13 different countries paraded into the stadium in Athens, Greece. With more than 70,000 spectators in the stands, the king of Greece declared the Games of the first modern Olympiad officially open.

The Opening and Closing Ceremonies have always been a highlight of the Olympic Games. Each host city stages a spectacular performance of music, dance, and special effects. Local citizens of all ages perform together to welcome the world to their city.

The Parade of Nations begins the opening ceremony. The Greek flag followed by Greece's athletes come first. Next comes the host country's flag and athletes, and then the remaining countries follow in alphabetical order.

Next, there are speeches by the president of the Organizing Committee and the president of the International Olympic Committee (IOC). The head of state officially declares the Games open. The Olympic flag is raised and the Olympic hymn is played. The Olympic torch is used to light the Olympic flame. Doves are released at this time as a symbol of peace. The Olympic Oath is taken by an athlete and an official. Cultural entertainment is provided by the host city.

Closing Ceremonies

After 17 days of competition, the Olympic athletes parade into the stadium, but not as countries. Athletes walk in together, competitors walking with competitors. This is done to symbolize the unity and friendship created because of the Games. Three flags are raised to the national anthems of Greece, the current host country, and the next host country. The Olympic flag is passed to the Mayor of the next host city. The president of the IOC pronounces the games closed. The Olympic flame is extinguished, the Olympic flag is lowered, the Olympic hymn played, and more cultural entertainment from the host city is presented.

Olympic Rings

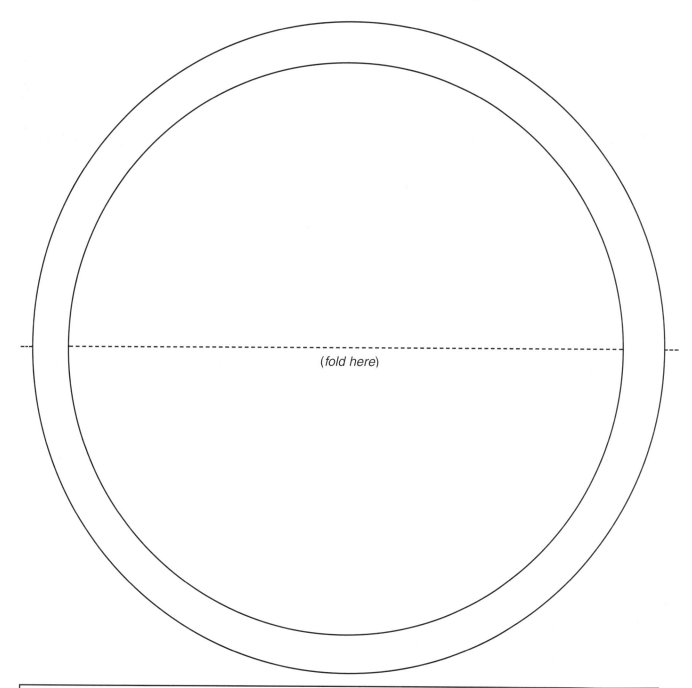

(*fold here*)

For younger students: Give each student one ring to color and cut out. To cut out, have students fold their papers on the dashed line. They then cut around the inside and outside of the circle. Students work together to assemble five rings of different colors together. You can assign students to a specific group and assign the color.

For older students: Make five copies of this page and instruct students to color the rings and use glue or tape to assemble the Olympic rings. Use these as decorations for your Opening and Closing Ceremonies.

Olympic Flag

Teacher Note: Have students cut out and glue this flag on to construction paper. These flags can be mounted on rulers to be carried, or they can be taped to a wall or bulletin board.

Olympic Flame

The Olympic torch is used to light the Olympic flame at the Opening Ceremonies. The Olympic flame will burn in a cauldron until the closing ceremonies. Draw a picture of the Olympic flame in the cauldron.

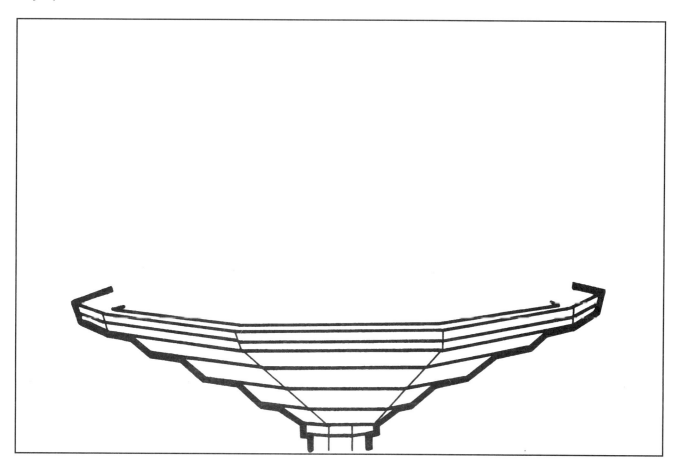

Write three rhyming words for each of the words below. On a separate piece of paper, use each of these rhyming words in a sentence. How many more rhyming words can you think of?

flame   **race**

_____   _____

_____   _____

_____   _____

torch   **jump**

_____   _____

_____   _____

_____   _____

Olympic Medals and Rewards

Have you ever won an award? Can you imagine winning a medal made of gold, silver, or bronze? This is a graph of how many medals these countries won at the 2000 Olympic Games.

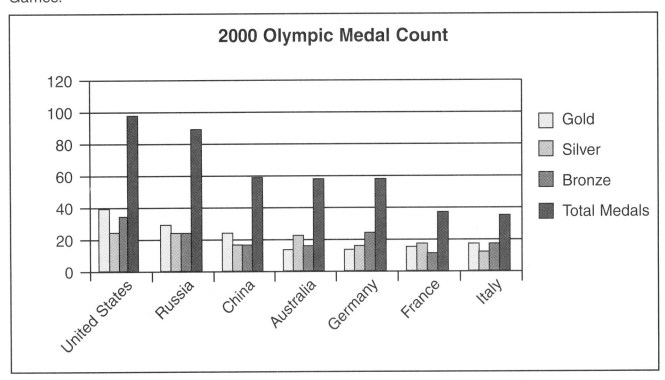

Use the graph above to answer these questions.

1. Which country won the most medals? _____

2. Which country won the least medals? _____

3. How many countries does this graph list? _____

4. Which three countries won about the same amount of medals?_____

5. Create your own question and answer it here:

   Question: _____

   _____

   Answer:_____

   _____

The Olympic Torch

Two months before the start of the Olympic Games, a torch is lit in Athens, Greece. The torch is carried by runners from country to country until it arrives at the Olympics. This torch is used to light the Olympic flame at the Opening Ceremonies.

Teacher Note: Have students color and cut out this Olympic torch. It can be attached to an empty paper towel holder with tape. Wrap the torch handle with aluminum foil. Students can carry their Olympic torches to the Opening Ceremonies of your Olympic Games.

Olympic Poetry

Poetry provides you with an opportunity to be creative. Write an Olympic poem using the three formats explained below.

➤ Acrostic Poems

This easy poem doesn't require rhyming! An acrostic poem has words written vertically. Then you use each letter in the word for the first letter of an adjective or phrase that describes the topic. Select a word about the Olympic Games and you are ready to begin! See the box to the right for an example of an acrostic poem.

> **O**nly the best athletes
> **L**et the games begin!
> **Y**ears of hard training
> **M**edals for the winners
> **P**ride in your accomplishments
> **I**t's the race of a lifetime
> **C**ompeting is an honor
> **S**ports for everyone!

➤ Sensory Poems

Can you imagine going to the Olympic Games? What would it look like? How would it smell? How would you feel? Use a poem to describe your feelings. Use the five senses combined with similes to create this "sense-sational" poem!

The Olympic Games look as _____ as a _____.

The Olympic Games smell as _____ as a _____.

The Olympic Games sound as _____ as a _____.

The Olympic Games taste as _____ as a _____.

The Olympic Games feel as _____ as a _____.

The Olympic Games are _____!

➤ The Newspaper Poem

The newspaper poem uses the 5 Ws as a guide. Each line of this poem answers one of the 5Ws you find in newspaper articles. These questions are *who, what, where, when,* and *why.* Brainstorm an Olympic topic to describe in your poem.

Who is the subject? ⟶ The athlete

What does he, she, or it do? ⟶ Runs the marathon

Where does he, she, or it do it? ⟶ In the Olympic Games

When does he, she, or it do it? ⟶ In the morning

Why does he, she, or it do it? ⟶ Because he is fast!

ABC Olympic Games

There are many words associated with the Olympic Games. Can you think of a word that goes with each letter of the alphabet? Write the words below. You can use the Olympic vocabulary words on page 12 as a reference, if necessary.

A _____   N _____

B _____   O _____

C _____   P _____

D _____   Q _____

E _____   R _____

F _____   S _____

G _____   T _____

H _____   U _____

I _____   V _____

J _____   W _____

K _____   X _____

L _____   Y _____

M _____   Z _____

For younger students: Work as a class to come up with a word for each letter of the alphabet. Next, distribute a piece of blank paper to each student. Assign each student a letter and the Olympic word. Write this word at the top of each paper. Then have the student illustrate a picture to accompany this word. If students are able, have them write a sentence about the pictures using their assigned word. Compile the alphabet pages in order and staple them to create a class alphabet book. Read this book as a class and store it in your class library for future reference.

For older students: Assign students to write a word for each letter of the alphabet. When finished, have students write a sentence for each word and draw a small illustration. If desired, students could make a small alphabet book using these Olympic words. (*Optional:* Arrange for students to read their alphabet Olympic books to younger students.)

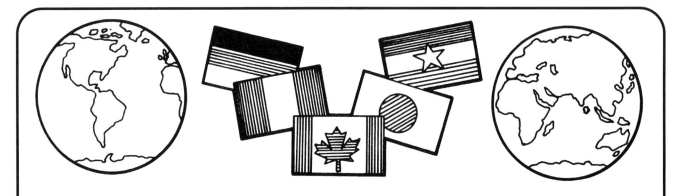

OLYMPIC VENUE
2

THE OLYMPIC SPIRIT THROUGHOUT THE WORLD

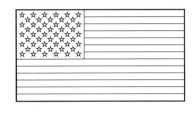

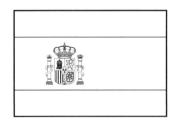

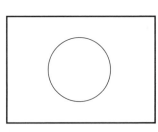

Olympic Host Cities

Through the years, many cities have hosted the Olympic Games and the Olympic Winter Games. Can you find these cities on a map? Use the map on pages 36 and 37. Instructions are on page 38.

Summer		Winter
Year	**City/Country**	**City/Country**
1896	Athens, Greece	*
1900	Paris, France	*
1904	St. Louis, MO, USA	*
1908	London, England	*
1912	Stockholm, Sweden	*
1916	Not Held (World War (I)	*
1920	Antwerp, Belgium	*
1924	Paris, France	Chamonix, France
1928	Amsterdam, The Netherlands	St. Moritz, Switzerland
1932	Los Angeles, CA, USA	Lake Placid, NY, USA
1936	Berlin, Germany	Garmisch-Patenkirchen, Germany
1940	not held (World War II)	not held (World War II)
1944	not held (World War II)	not held (World War II)
1948	London, England	St. Moritz, Switzerland
1952	Helsinki, Finland	Oslo, Norway
1956	Melbourne, Australia	Cortina, Italy
1960	Rome, Italy	Squaw Valley, CA, USA
1964	Tokyo, Japan	Innsbruck, Austria
1968	Mexico City, Mexico	Grenoble, France
1972	Munich, West Germany	Sapporo, Japan
1976	Montreal, Canada	Innsbruck, Austria
1980	Moscow, Russia	Lake Placid, NY, USA
1984	Los Angeles, CA, USA	Sarajevo, Yugoslavia
1988	Seoul, South Korea	Calgary, Canada
1992	Barcelona, Spain	Albertville, France
1996	Atlanta, GA, USA	Lillehammer, Norway (1994)**
2000	Sydney, Australia	Nagano, Japan (1998)**
2004	Athens, Greece	Salt Lake City, USA (2002)**

* Olympic Winter Games began in 1924.

** It was decided in 1992 to alternate the Olympic Games and the Olympic Winter Games every two years. This new schedule began in 1994.

World Map

Use the tab to connect pages 36 and 37.

World Map *(cont.)*

Continents of the World

Materials:

- globe

- copy of "World Map," with continents listed (pages 36–37) for each student

- transparency of "World Map" (pages 36–37)

- white board and white-board markers

- overhead projector

- crayons or colored pencils

Directions:

1. Explain to students that countries from all over the world come to compete in the Olympic Games. Each of these countries represents a continent.

2. Place the transparency of the world map on the overhead projector. Display this transparency on the white board. Explain to students that all of the countries of the world are represented on this map.

3. Distribute individual copies of this map to students. Have the students locate on their maps what you locate on the map displayed on the white board. Have crayons or colored pencils available for students.

4. Show students the large portions of land on the overhead map. Explain to students that these large portions of land are called continents. The names of the continents in the world are:

Australia ➔ *green*	**Europe** ➔ *blue*
North America ➔ *red*	**Africa** ➔ *purple*
South America ➔ *orange*	**Antarctica** ➔ *brown*
Asia ➔ *yellow*	

5. Fill in the continent of Australia with green. (Assign each continent a color so that students won't be confused.) Now identify, label, and color the rest of the continents.

6. Explain that countries are located on continents. One continent can have many countries. For example, the continent of North America includes the countries of Canada, the United States of America, and Mexico.

7. Now, show students the globe. Explain to students that this is a map of the world on a sphere. Help students identify and locate the continents on the globe. (Do this the following day with younger students.)

Olympic Countries

The flags on pages 39 and 40 are from some of the countries that have hosted the Olympic Games. Follow the directions to color each flag. You will be selecting one of these countries to research further.

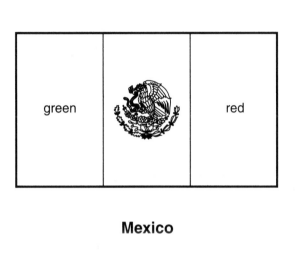

Mexico

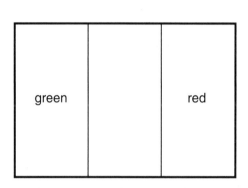

Italy

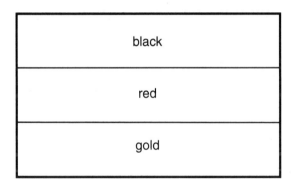

Germany

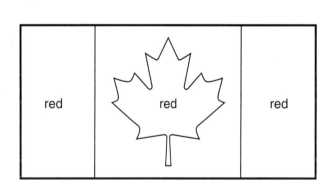

Canada

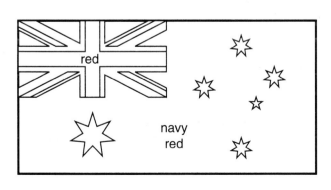

Australia

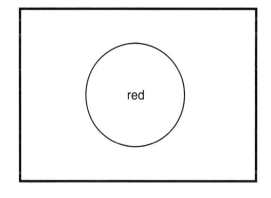

Japan

Olympic Countries *(cont.)*

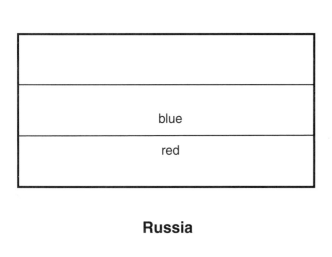

Russia

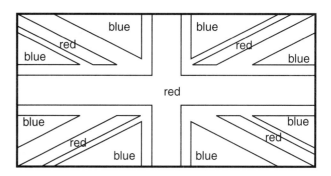

Great Britain

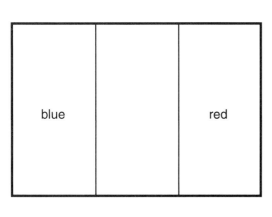

France

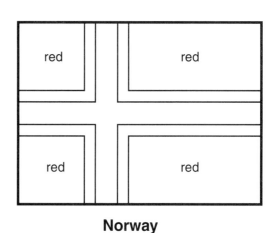

Norway

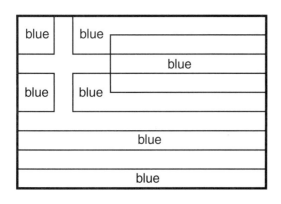

Greece

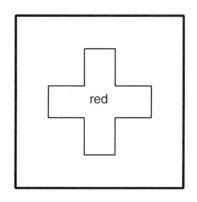

Switzerland

Country K-W-L

Once you have selected a country of the Olympic Games to research, you are ready to begin. What do you already know about this country? What do you want to know? Are you ready to learn? Fill out the graphic organizer below to organize your previous knowledge and other information. Keep this page handy as you will refer to it later.

K	W	L
Things I already *know* about this country	**Things I *want* to learn about this country**	**Things I have *learned* about this country**

Teacher Note: Demonstrate how to complete the KWL chart for your class. Select a country to use for the KWL chart. Call on students to help generate what they know and want to know about this country. Explain to students that after they have finished researching, they will need to go back and change inaccurate information and add the things they have learned. Younger students can draw pictures instead of writing, if necessary.

Research an Olympic Country

Select one of the countries that has participated in or has hosted the Olympic Games. Research this country using books, pamphlets, brochures, magazines, newspapers, encyclopedias, and other resources provided by your teacher.

My Country: _____

Cities in this country: _____

_____

_____

Foods: _____

_____

_____

Clothing: _____

_____

_____

Plants and animals: _____

_____

_____

Teacher Note: For younger students, assign students to work in small groups that study one country. Provide picture books for students to use as a resource. Students work together to complete this page. Students can draw pictures, if necessary.

Research an Olympic Country *(cont.)*

Teacher Note: You will be setting up an Olympic Countries Museum. This museum will be a display for students to teach and learn from each other. This museum could be shared with other classes as well, and this would give students another opportunity to share their findings and research. Be sure to have enough tables or desks available to hold the museum exhibits.

For younger students: Let them help you set up the displays. Ask students to illustrate pictures and maps.

For older students: They can work with a partner to put together a museum exhibit for their country.

Option A: Museum Exhibit

Now that you have gathered information about your country, you are ready to share your findings. You will be required to set up a museum exhibit on your country. Be sure to have something representing each of the topics you researched. Here are some ideas you can use:

- map of your country
- flag
- artifacts
- sample music
- recipes
- costumes
- currency
- pictures of the land, people, vegetation
- Olympic moments, memories, athletes

Teacher Note: If you feel that you do not have the space for a museum, you can select Option B for students to share the findings and research of their counties.

Option B: Country Presentation

You are also required to give an oral presentation on the country you researched. There are various ways you can present the information you have gathered. You may use one of the following suggestions or one of your own as long as it is approved by the teacher:

- Draw pictures to hold up as you speak.
- Paint pictures of your country.
- Create a 3-D model of your country.
- Create a large mural of your country.
- Create a diorama of your country.
- Write a journal of an imaginary sight-seeing trip to your country.
- Put together an informative newscast of your country.

The Olympic Games and the World

Directions: Count the letters in each word.

1. Circle the shortest word.

   Spain   **France**   **Russia**   **Germany**   **Canada**

2. Circle the continent that has a different first letter than the others.

   Africa   **Asia**   **Europe**   **Australia**

3. Circle the word that has a different last letter than the others.

   Italy   **Spain**   **Japan**   **Sweden**

4. Circle the word that begins with a vowel.

   Brazil   **Guatemala**   **Greece**   **Argentina**

5. Circle the country that begins with the second letter of the alphabet.

   Mexico   **Belgium**   **Canada**   **Israel**   **Portugal**

6. Circle the country that begins with a consonant.

   U.S.A.   **Argentina**   **Netherlands**   **Ecuador**

7. Circle the longest word.

   cultural   **continent**   **money**   **traditions**

For younger students: Follow the directions as stated.

For older students: Follow the directions. Then write a sentence using one of the words from each group.

Olympic-Sized Problems

You will be working in a small group for this activity. Read the problems below, and then discuss a possible solution to resolve the conflict. Select one member of the group to be the recorder. Have the recorder write down the solutions. Be prepared to share your answers with the class.

Conflict A

Several athletes from different countries have been assigned to room next door to each other in the Olympic Village. Athletes from one country like to get up very early in the morning, and they wake up other athletes. Some athletes want to sleep more to get their rest. What do you think should be done? _____

_____

_____

_____

Conflict B

It is important to keep our bodies clean and healthy. There are some substances that athletes are not allowed to use to help them run faster. Some athletes think they need to use drugs that make them stronger or faster but are bad for their bodies. What do you think should be done if one of the competing athletes has been caught using these drugs? _____

_____

_____

_____

Conflict C

Two countries have been fighting with each other before the Olympic Games. These two teams are scheduled to play the first soccer game of the Olympic Games. What must Olympic officials do to make sure that everyone will get along and be safe during the game?

_____

_____

_____

Conflict D

The U.S. Gymnastics team will be competing as a team, as well as individually in the individual competition. How can the teammates work together towards a common goal, as well as compete against each other?_____

_____

_____

_____

Olympic Nouns and Verbs

In each box, draw a picture that matches the sentence. Underline the nouns in each sentence. Identify each noun as a person, place, or thing.

The athlete throws the javelin.	The woman swings the bat as hard as she can.
The diver dives into the deep pool.	The man rides the horse across the finish line.

Extension: Write a sentence and have a classmate draw a picture to illustrate it. Can your classmate identify and label the types of nouns used in your sentence?

Teacher Note: For younger students, have them just draw a picture in each box that matches the sentence.

What Does It Say?

Directions: Add or subtract. Each answer has a letter. Put the letters on the lines that match the answers. You will find the Olympic Motto. A few letters have been solved for you.

1. $1 - 1 =$ ___0___	S	11. $3 + 1 =$ _____	G
2. $4 + 4 =$ ___8___	H	12. $0 + 8 =$ _____	H
3. $2 - 1 =$ _____	R	13. $5 + 4 =$ _____	O
4. $5 - 1 =$ _____	G	14. $2 + 3 =$ _____	T
5. $2 + 1 =$ _____	I	15. $2 + 4 =$ _____	W
6. $10 - 5 =$ _____	T	16. $5 - 4 =$ _____	R
7. $8 - 1 =$ _____	F	17. $8 - 6 =$ _____	E
8. $1 + 1 =$ _____	E	18. $10 - 9 =$ _____	R
9. $6 - 5 =$ _____	R	19. $7 - 4 =$ _____	I
10. $6 + 4 =$ _____	N	20. $6 - 4 =$ _____	E

Bonus: What is the Olympic Motto?

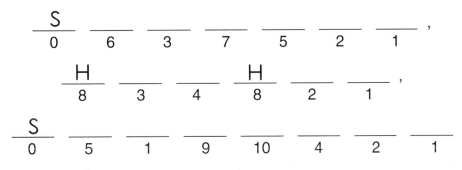

$$\underset{0}{\text{S}} \ \underset{6}{\quad} \ \underset{3}{\quad} \ \underset{7}{\quad} \ \underset{5}{\quad} \ \underset{2}{\quad} \ \underset{1}{\quad} \ ,$$

$$\underset{8}{\text{H}} \ \underset{3}{\quad} \ \underset{4}{\quad} \ \underset{8}{\text{H}} \ \underset{2}{\quad} \ \underset{1}{\quad} \ ,$$

$$\underset{0}{\text{S}} \ \underset{5}{\quad} \ \underset{1}{\quad} \ \underset{9}{\quad} \ \underset{10}{\quad} \ \underset{4}{\quad} \ \underset{2}{\quad} \ \underset{1}{\quad}$$

47

What Is the Metric System?

The metric system is used at the Olympic Games to measure distance. This activity will let you practice using the metric system.

The Metric Scavenger Hunt

Can you locate objects in your classroom that are these measurements? Remember that the abbreviation for centimeters is *cm*.

Metric Lengths	Name of Object	Actual Measurement
1. 87 cm		
2. 5 cm		
3. 240 cm		
4. 66 cm		
5. 1 cm		
6. 17 cm		
7. 10 cm		
8. 112 cm		

For younger students: Show students a meter stick. Select an object in your room to measure. Measure the object in centimeters. Ask students to locate something in the room that is about the same length. Using a ruler, check to see how close the student's guess is. Now measure another object in the room. Encourage students to locate an item of similar length, using centimeters. If time permits, and you feel the students are ready, give them rulers to "practice" measuring using centimeters.

For older students: Have students work with a partner to locate objects in your classroom that are close to the measurements in the scavenger hunt below. Each pair of students will need a meter stick to locate the items.

Metric Games

Directions: This activity will give students a first-hand experience using the metric system, but it will require adult volunteers! You can do this activity in place of learning centers. Divide your class into groups of four or five. Set up a station for each of the Metric Olympic events. Be sure that all the materials needed at each event/station are available. With adult help, students will record their results on the space indicated. You can also invite an older class to come and assist your class with this project. Students can work with a buddy. Assign each groups a starting station. Students will rotate through the events/stations. All measurements should be made using metric units. Make a copy of this page for each student so that you can record measurements for each student. **Note:** Always use caution when doing these activities. Keep the area in front of and around the student athletes clear to prevent accidents.

Materials Needed

- paper plates (4 to 5)
- paper straws (4 to 5)
- cotton balls
- masking tape

- meter sticks (1 for each pair of students, if possible)
- small rulers with metric measurements (1 for each pair of students, if possible)

Standing Long Jump

At this station, make a line with masking tape. Students are to stand on the line and do a standing long jump. Students are allowed two jumps. The longest jump counts.

➢ First Jump   Distance:_____

➢ Second Jump   Distance:_____

Paper Plate Discus

At this event, mark a line with masking tape. Students stand on the line and throw the paper plate like a Frisbee. Students measure the distance the paper plate traveled. Students have two tries to throw the Frisbee. The longest throw counts.

➢ First Throw   Distance:_____

➢ Second Throw   Distance:_____

Straw Javelin Throw

This event is set up like the paper plate discus, except the students will be throwing a straw javelin. Students have two throws. The longest throw counts.

➢ First Throw   Distance:_____

➢ Second Throw   Distance:_____

Cotton Ball Shot Put

This event is set up like the paper plate discus, except that students will be using the cotton ball as a shot put. Students have two shot puts. The longest shot counts.

➢ First Throw   Distance:_____

➢ Second Throw   Distance:_____

In the Zone

Look at the list of words in the word box. All of these words are nouns. Some of them are places, some are people, and some are things. Write each word under the correct heading.

Noun Word Box		
judge	Italy	France
ball	race	athlete
coach	Germany	Greece
spectator	United States	winner
medal	flag	torch

People

_____

_____

_____

_____

Places

_____

_____

_____

_____

Things

_____

_____

_____

_____

_____

Teacher Note: For younger students, you will need to complete this activity as a class. Help your students locate the people, places, and things. Model for students how to write these words in the proper place. You can make a transparency of this page and display it on an overhead projector for students to see.

Compounding the Games

There are many compound words that can be found when studying the Olympic Games. Read the word in the center. Can you draw a picture for each part of the compound word? Now cut your pictures and exchange them with a partner. Can he or she put your compound words together?

base + ball

snow + board

basket + ball

hand + ball

Olympic Learning Centers

This page lists center suggestions that can be used to reinforce skills taught and discussed in the classroom. Select the centers that you think would best meet the needs of your students.

Math Center

- Have clipboards, paper, and pencils available for students to tally up the number of sports equipment or other items found in the classroom that might be used at the Olympic Games that they can find in the classroom. How many balls are there? Is there a whistle? How many students in the class like to run? Is there a stopwatch in the classroom?

Reading Center

- Set up an area in your room for independent reading. Place beanbags, pillows, or chairs for more comfort. Keep a bookshelf of books available at all times for student to read and browse. For this center, have books available for students about the Olympic Games. (See bibliography on page 96.)

- Create sentence strips from the Olympic mini-books (see Venue 1). At this center, have students work together to read the sentences and figure out the sequence of the sentences. Have a little book of this story available for students to check their work or to use as needed.

Writing Center

- Allow time for students to write in their literacy journals. Be sure to have a literacy journal available for each student with his or her name on it. A literacy journal can be made by stapling lined paper inside a cover. A journal can also be made with a notebook. You can have pre-assigned topics for students to write about or leave it up to the students. Encourage students to write or draw picture about the Olympic Games. What are they learning about the Olympic Games? What would it be like to be an Olympic athlete?

- Assign each student a letter of the alphabet. At this center, students will illustrate a picture of something from the Olympic Games that begins with the letter they have been assigned. At the end, put all of the pages in order and bind them to make a class book. Share this book with the class and acknowledge each student for his or her contribution. You may have to get creative for those hard to think of letters like *q, x, y,* or *z.*

Art Center

- Set up an easel with paper. Have students use watercolor paints to paint pictures of athletes participating in the Olympic Games. You can also have the Olympic mini-books available for students to illustrate the sentences from the book. Hang the illustrations around the room when paintings are dry. Students can sequence the illustrations by placing them in order.

Dramatic Play Center

- Set up a center for students to try on sport uniforms. Don't have equipment with wheels or bats, etc., at this center as students might get hurt. Focus on the uniforms and let students pretend with their hands and feet.

OLYMPIC VENUE
3

THE OLYMPIC ATHLETE AND OLYMPIC SPORTS

Match the Sports

In which sports and events do Olympic athletes compete in the Olympic Games? The International Olympic Committee chooses the sports for each Olympic Games. There are different sports and events for the Olympic Games and the Olympic Winter Games. Prior to this activity, you will need to discuss each of the pictograms and the sports represented on them. If possible, you can have sports equipment available to show students.

Directions:

1. Make copies of Olympic pictograms on pages 56–60.

2. Cut out the pictograms. Be sure to cut off the name of the sport. Write the name of the sport on the back of each pictogram for later use. You will need a set of pictograms for each group of students.

3. Divide students into groups, or pair them with a partner. Give each group a set of pictograms. Have students read through the list of Olympic sports and see if they can locate the pictogram that goes with that sport. Students will need a large work area to do this.

4. First, match the pictogram with the Olympic Winter Games on this page and then do the same for the Olympic Games on page 55.

5. You may wish to play a game of Concentration with the pictograms and cards. Place all cards and pictograms facedown. Each student picks one pictogram and one card. If they match, the student keeps them; if not, the cards and pictograms are returned to their facedown position. The student with the most cards at the end wins the game.

Olympic Winter Games Events

Biathlon	Curling	Ice Hockey
Speed Skating	Bobsled	Luge
Skiing	Figure Skating	Snowboarding

Match the Sports *(cont.)*

Match the Olympic pictograms on pages 57–60 with the Olympic summer events.

Olympic Games Events

Archery	Judo	Table Tennis
Athletics	Modern Pentathlon	Taekwondo
Badminton	Rowing	Tennis
Baseball	Sailing	Triathlon
Basketball	Shooting	Team Handball
Boxing	Soccer	Volleyball
Canoe/Kayaking	Softball	Weightlifting
Gymnastics	Swimming	Water Polo
Equestrian	Synchronized Swimming	Wrestling
Field Hockey		

Olympic Pictograms

Winter Sports

Biathlon

Curling

Ice Hockey

Bobsled

Figure Skating

Luge

Skiing

Snowboarding

Speed Skating

Olympic Pictograms *(cont.)*

Summer Sports

Archery

Athletics

Badminton

Baseball

Basketball

Boxing

Canoeing/Kayaking

Cycling

Olympic Pictograms *(cont.)*

Summer Sports *(cont.)*

Diving

Fencing

Gymnastics

Equestrian

Field Hockey

Judo

Modern Pentathlon

Rowing

Olympic Pictograms *(cont.)*

Summer Sports *(cont.)*

Sailing

Shooting

Soccer

Softball

Swimming

Synchronized Swimming

Table Tennis

Taekwondo

Olympic Pictograms *(cont.)*

Summer Sports *(cont.)*

Team Handball

Tennis

Triathlon

Volleyball

Weightlifting

Water Polo

Wrestling

Comparing the Games

The Olympic Winter Games made their debut in 1924. The first Olympic Winter Games were held in Chamonix, France. What is the difference between the Olympic Games and the Olympic Winter Games? Use the Venn diagram below to list the similarities and differences. Place the similarities in the center where the two circles connect. *For younger students, you will need to do the Venn diagram together as a class.*

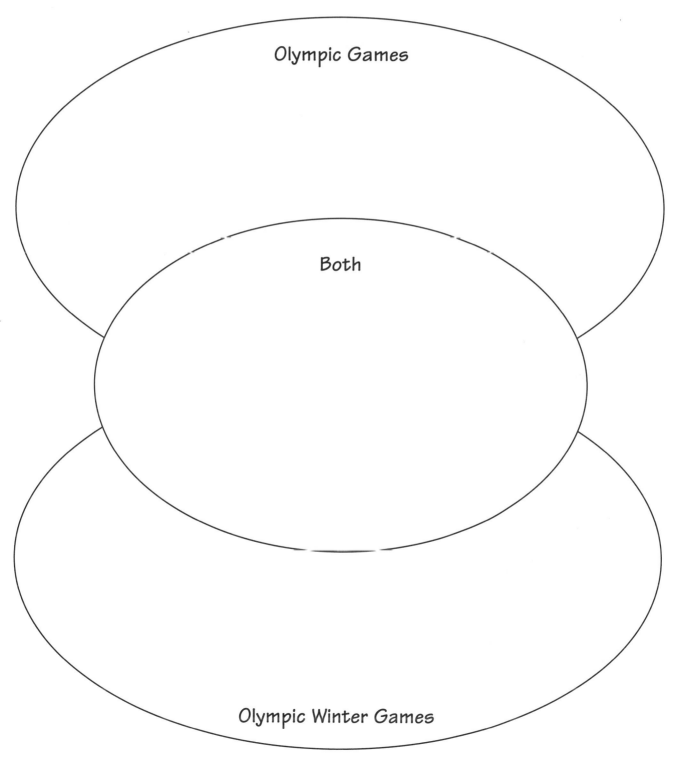

Olympic Games

Both

Olympic Winter Games

Olympic Sports

Using the pictograms from pages 56–60, glue the pictures under the correct headings. (Not all of the pictograms need to be used.) On the back of this paper, write a paragraph about an experience you have had with an Olympic sport.

Olympic Sports I Play	Olympic Sports I Watch

Teacher Note: For younger students, write a sentence about your favorite Olympic sport.

It's All in a Word

1. Circle the word that begins with a vowel.

   dive   **jump**   **swim**   **run**   **aim**

2. Circle the shortest word.

   badminton   **taekwando**   **basketball**   **volleyball**   **softball**

3. Circle the word that has a different number of letters than the others.

   pentathlon   **volleyball**   **basketball**   **equestrian**   **taekwando**

4. Circle the longest word.

   swimming   **running**   **fencing**   **jumping**   **cycling**

5. Circle the word that ends with a different letter than the others do.

   handball   **softball**   **athletics**   **basketball**   **volleyball**

6. Circle the word that begins with a consonant.

   target   **aim**   **arch**   **over**   **equestrian**

For younger students: Read each set of directions to the students. Have them write the number of letters under each word.

For older students: Ask students to choose five words from this page and then write a sentence for each of these words.

Famous Olympic Athletes

Below is a list of former Olympic athletes. Select one of these athletes to study and write the sport or event that you think this athlete competed in on the line. Research information about this athlete and how he or she accomplished the Olympic dream. Check with your teacher to see that no one else has selected this athlete to study. Use the following page to organize your findings.

❑ Abbott, Jim _____

❑ Biondi, Matt _____

❑ Blair, Bonnie _____

❑ Boitano, Brian _____

❑ Button, Dick _____

❑ Comaneci, Nadia _____

❑ deVarona, Donna _____

❑ Evans, Janet _____

❑ Fleming, Peggy _____

❑ Foreman, George _____

❑ Griffith-Joyner, Florence _____

❑ Hamill, Dorothy _____

❑ Hamilton, Scott _____

❑ Heiden, Eric _____

❑ Jansen, Dan _____

❑ Jenner, Bruce _____

❑ Joyner-Kersee, Jackie _____

❑ Kerrigan, Nancy _____

❑ Lewis, Carl _____

❑ Lipinski, Tara _____

❑ Louganis, Greg _____

❑ Miller, Shannon _____

❑ O'Brien, Dan _____

❑ Owens, Jesse _____

❑ Retton, Mary Lou _____

❑ Thorpe, Jim _____

❑ Witt, Katerina _____

❑ Yamaguchi, Kristy _____

For younger students: Work as a class to study a few of the Olympic Games names on this page. Collect books, Internet articles, and other resources for students to "gather research." Encourage students to tell you what they have learned about the athletes. Fill in page 65 for each athlete studied as a class.

For older students: Have students work individually or with a partner to study and research the accomplishment of one of the athletes on this page. Use page 65 to record the research. Allow time in class for students to share their work.

Researching an Athlete

Select an Olympic athlete that you would like to research (page 64). Once you have chosen your Olympic athlete, you are ready to begin. Use this page to organize your research and information.

Name:

Date of birth:

Place of birth:

Competing/competed for this country:

Language spoken:

Sport/athletic event:

Background/experience: _____

_____

_____

Career highlights/interesting information: _____

_____

_____

_____

_____

Olympic Hall of Fame

Draw a picture of your athlete in his/her sport and post it on an "Olympic Hall of Fame" bulletin board.

Name of Athlete: _____ Country: _____

Things about this athlete: _____

_____

_____

_____

_____

A Tale Told of an Athlete

Embedded in the history of the Olympic Games are stories that portray commitment, courage, dedication, honor, strength, fitness, and more. Read these inspirational Olympic stories to your students.

Luz Long and Jesse Owens

Jesse Owens was an African American who competed in the 1936 Olympic Games. Many people back then believed that an African American wouldn't be able to compete very well. One of these people was Adolf Hitler. He wanted to prove that his people were better than other people. One of his athletes was Luz Long. Long was a white German long jumper, and he was very good. Jesse Owens had already won a gold medal in the 100-meter dash and was competing against Long in the long jump.

Jesse Owens, however, was having a hard time trying to qualify in the long jump finals. He thought he was taking a practice run, but found out that it was his first jump. He was upset and messed up on his second jump. With only one jump to go, Luz Long tapped Owens on the shoulder and told him to move his mark back a foot and not to try and hit the take-off board. With Luz Long's advice, Jesse Owens qualified and went on to win the finals. He managed to set a new Olympic record of over 26 feet.

Sonja Henie

Women have found their place in Olympic history, as well. Sonja Henie was the first superstar of women's figure skating. Sonja was born in Oslo, Norway, on April 8, 1912. In 1924 she competed in the Olympic Winter Games as an 11-year-old. She finished last out of eight competitors, but she got better and better. By the 1926 World Championships, she finished second. From then on for the next 10 years, she won first place each year at the World Championships.

Sonja Henie went on to win gold medals at the 1928, 1932, and 1936 Olympic Winter Games. Sonja turned professional in 1936. She was asked to star in movies and soon became very wealthy. She acted in ten feature films and introduced flair to the world of figure skating. Sonja toured the world performing in ice reviews and dazzling the crowds. She became one of the richest athletes ever. She later suffered from leukemia and died during a flight from Paris, France, to Oslo, Norway. The world will always remember Sonja Henie and her style on ice.

================ **Questions to Consider** ================

1. What is an *obstacle?*

2. How do you think these athletes overcame their obstacles?

3. Do you have obstacles in your life?

4. What obstacles did these athletes have to face?

5. What made these athletes great?

Obstacles to Success

Read each question. Think before answering the following questions. Answer these questions on a separate piece of paper.

1. Define greatness. What is it? What does it look like? _____

_____

2. What makes an Olympic athlete great? _____

_____

3. What do you think motivates a great Olympic athlete? _____

_____

4. Define the word *obstacle*. What is it? What does an obstacle look like?_____

_____

5. List any obstacles that an Olympic athlete might have to face. _____

_____

6. Did the Olympic athlete you studied have to overcome any obstacles? What were they?

_____

_____

7. Now, look at yourself. What makes you great? What qualities and talents do you possess? _____

_____

8. What goals do you have? List at least five._____

_____

9. What obstacles might prevent you from accomplishing your goals? _____

_____

10. What can you do to overcome these obstacles? Tell about your plan._____

_____

_____

11. How will you know what success looks like? On the back of this paper, write a paragraph (or more) about a personal experience you have had with a goal, an obstacle, and finally success. Remember a narrative is written in first person sharing a personal experience. Check your spelling, punctuation, and handwriting. Make it great!

Teacher Note: For younger students, read the questions. Discuss these questions as a class.

Letter to an Olympic Athlete

Select an Olympic athlete from the past or present that you admire. If you could send a letter to this person, what would you say? Read the sample letter below. On a separate piece of paper, write your own imaginary letter to the Olympic athlete you have chosen. Don't forget to use the parts of a letter. These parts are the date, the address, greeting, body of the letter, closing, and signature.

September 16, 2005

Clifton Cushman
1349 Hidden Canyon Road
Los Angeles, CA 98674

Dear Mr. Cushman,

I have just read an article about your experience competing for the 1964 Olympic team. I bet you were frustrated and upset when you fell during the hurdle race, but your example after the race is even more important to young people like me.

Thanks for setting a good example for us and letting us know that winning isn't everything. You are an amazing athlete! I can't believe what you were able to do.

I want you to know that I have a lot of respect and admiration for you. I wish I could tell you how impressed I am with your ability to keep giving it your best! Keep up the great work! I am one of your biggest fans.

Sincerely,

Jane Jensen

Jane Jensen

Teacher Note: You will need to help younger students write this letter. You can model how to write a letter and assist with spelling, if necessary.

Create an Olympic Sport

Olympic sports and events are added to the Olympic Games all the time. Create an Olympic sport that you think would be popular. Answer the questions to describe your creation. Remember, this must be a sport or event never seen at the Olympic Games before.

1. What is the name of your sport/event? _____

_____

2. What is the objective of your sport/event? _____

_____

3. What are the rules and directions needed to participate in this sport/event?

_____

_____

4. What uniform or equipment would athletes need to compete in this sport/event?

_____

_____

5. What judges or officials will be needed to help run this sport/event? _____

_____

6. Describe the scoring system for this sport/event? _____

_____

7. Draw a picture of athlete(s) competing in your sport/event

Games on Ice

Did you know that all of the Winter Olympic sports require snow or ice? How is an athlete able to move quickly across the ice or in the snow? How does an athlete stop on ice or snow? Ice and snow are made of water. Use this page to demonstrate for your students how ice is made and how it can be used to create some of the most popular Olympic sports to watch.

Water is one of the few known substances that naturally exists on Earth as a gas (otherwise known as *vapor*), a solid, and a liquid.

gas = *vapor*   **solid** = *ice*   **liquid** = *water*

1. Show water in the different forms and stages. You can show water as a vapor by heating a pot of water on a hot plate. The steam rising off the top is the vapor. Pour water into an ice tray and have the students put it in a freezer. Pull it out later to check the process of freezing. Pull it out the next day to show the solid ice.

2. Ice is a unique solid because it has very little friction. This lack of friction allows things to slide and is a requirement for all Winter Olympic sports. To demonstrate this, freeze a thin layer of water in a cookie sheet. Have the students take turns trying to slide a penny across the ice, across a piece of carpeting, across a piece of sandpaper, and across their desktops. They will discover that the penny glides the easiest (the farthest) on the ice.

3. Discuss friction with your students. *Friction* is a force trying to stop movement between two surfaces. Which of the surfaces from question #2 had the most friction? Why do you think so? Which surface had the least friction? Why do you think this is?

4. When something moves across ice, its weight pushes down on the ice and makes it temporarily melt. This reduces friction and enables skaters, bobsled runners, and luge sleds to glide over the ice quickly. The ice melts under the runners of the skates or sled. As soon as the weight passes over, the ice refreezes if the temperature is low enough.

5. Ask students to predict what will happen when ice cubes melt. Use a glass filled with ice cubes. Most will think the glass will overflow. Set a glass with ice aside and check it later in the day when the ice has completely melted. Explain that it did not overflow because the water from the ice takes up less space than the ice cube did.

6. If possible, show a video of a figure skater gliding across the ice and a skier skiing down a mountain. How does the skater stop and start? How does the skier use the skis to stop and start? What makes the skis go down the hill faster? Slower?

Extension: Invite an athlete who participates in winter sports to your class. Ask the athlete to share what it feels like to move on ice or snow. What makes it difficult?

You Be the Judge

In every Olympic Games, the work of judges is very important. In somes sports, their opinion determines the medal. Racing events were judged by eye until 1912 Olympic Games when the electrical timing device was introduced. The 1932 Los Angeles Games brought electronic scoring. Today, measuring devices are very accurate. The difference between a gold and silver medal can be measured in a few hundredths of a second.

Look at the pictures below. Cut the pictures out and put them in order of what happened first to last.

OLYMPIC VENUE

4

THE OLYMPIC EXPERIENCE IN YOUR SCHOOL

The Olympic Experience

As a culminating activity for your students, you are now ready to move to the last venue. Venue 4 is putting on the Olympic Games in your school. This can be done as a class or as a school. These directions are for hosting the Olympic Games as a class. (See pages 89–90 for instructions on how to adapt this activity for a school-wide experience.) Don't forget to have students add their Venue 4 stickers to their Olympic Passport when the Class Olympic Games are completed.

Your students will have fun staging their own Olympic Games. This will take dedication, hard work, and adult volunteers. Each student will be involved in competing and organizing the Olympic Games. Each student will be placed on a team and a committee. The directions and instructions needed to stage these Olympic Games will follow on the next few pages of this unit. Below is a suggested map of how to set up these Olympic Games.

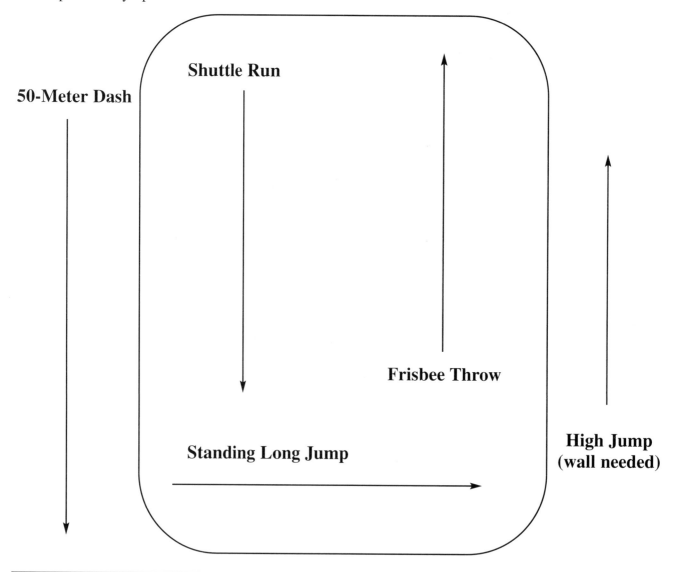

Teacher Note: The Academic Olympic Games will take place indoors. They can be held in your classroom.

Creating a Team

Divide your class into groups of five students. It will work best if there are no more than five teams in your classroom. If you have more than 25 students, you can add to the teams. The teams should be as equal as possible. Be sure to take academic and athletic ability into consideration when forming teams. The teams should have a nice balance. Once the teams have been created, they are ready to get organized!

Team Name

Each team needs a name. Have students work together to brainstorm names and determine the name for their team. The team can have a mascot, if desired.

Team Color

Each team will be assigned a color. The colors correspond to the rings on the Olympic flag. Students will want to use this color to create team identity.

➤ **Red**   *Team 1*   Team name: _____

➤ **Yellow**   *Team 2*   Team name: _____

➤ **Black**   *Team 3*   Team name: _____

➤ **Blue**   *Team 4*   Team name: _____

➤ **Green**   *Team 5*   Team name: _____

At the Opening Ceremonies, each team will be required to wear their team color. This will help identify who belongs on what team.

Team Flag

Once the team name and color has been established, teams are ready to design and create a team flag. Teams can put their mascot on their flag. Using white construction paper (or white material) and colored markers, students can make their flags. They will need one large flag to carry into the Opening Ceremonies, and they can make smaller flags for each team member to use, as well. When the flags are completed, mount them on wooden dowels so they are easy to carry. Make sure that all the official team flags are the same size.

Team Cheer

Team members should work together to come up with a team cheer. This cheer will be used to encourage and cheer on team members while they are competing at the Olympic Games.

The Olympic Torch

As a team, have students work together to make torches. These torches can be carried at the Opening Ceremonies, as well. A torch can be made by coloring the pattern on page 31, or students can make a torch by fastening a crumpled piece of orange tissue paper inside an empty paper-towel tube.

Olympic Day Schedule

There are two parts of the Olympic Games: the Athletic Olympic Games and the Academic Olympic Games. This schedule lists both of these in one day. You may choose to hold the Athletic Olympic Games one day and the Academic Olympic Games the next. Feel free to make adjustments in the times, the events, and the schedule. This is a sample schedule only. Descriptions of the individual and team events are on pages 77–79.

8:30 A.M.	Opening Ceremonies
	Individual Events *(Students will participate in one event only)*
9:00 A.M.	Boys' 50-meter dash
	Girls' 50-meter dash
9:30 A.M.	Girls' Frisbee Throw
	Boys' Frisbee Throw
10:00 A.M.	Boy's Standing Long Jump
	Girls' Standing Long Jump
10:30 A.M.	Girls' High Jump
	Boys' High Jump
11:00 A.M.	Boys' Shuttle Run
	Girls' Shuttle Run
11:30 A.M.	Lunch Break
	Team Events *(All students will compete in teams)*
12:00 P.M.	Boys' 4 x 50-meter relay (4 members per team—1 member cheers)
	Girls' 4 x 50-meter relay (4 members per team—1 member cheers)
12:30 P.M.	Soccer Game *(All members of each team participate.)*
1:30 P.M.	Academic Olympic Games *(See page 82 for directions.)*
2:00 P.M.	Awards Ceremony and Closing Ceremonies

**Remember: When the day is done, have your students record their experiences in their Olympic Journal entry on page 94.

Extension: You may wish to try other games and events. Other athletic-event suggestions include a volleyball game, swimming races, basketball game, kickball game, three-legged races, and other running races. You could also host an Olympic Games featuring the Olympic sports and events created by the students.

Athletic Olympic Event Descriptions

Individual Events

❖ 50-Meter Dash

(For younger students, you may choose to do shorter distance or do practice runs to prepare your students.)

Materials Needed: measuring tape, cones indicating start and finish line, stopwatches, whistle, flag (*optional*), event record sheet (page 81), pencil

Directions: Using the measuring tape, measure off 50 meters on your playground or field. For the most accurate results, each runner will have to run and be timed individually. If time does not allow this, you can have a group of runners and have a volunteer time each runner. If you do not have a stopwatch, you may start all of the runners at the same time and make a visual judgement about the first three finishers. The whistle can be the sound for the runners to "go." The flag can be waved as the runners cross the finish line. The three athletes with the fastest runs will be awarded the gold, silver, and bronze medals.

Help Needed: This event will need a volunteer at the starting line explaining to the runners where they are running and how they will start the race. This volunteer will work closely with the volunteers at the finish line. At the finish line, you will need a stopwatch and volunteer for each runner.

❖ Frisbee Throw

Materials Needed: masking tape to mark the starting point, five or more Frisbees, a measuring tape, event record sheet (page 81), pencil, and marker

Directions: Each athlete stands on the starting point and throws the Frisbee as far as he or she can. The athlete is not allowed to get a running start. Judges in the field use masking tape to mark the landing spot of each Frisbee. The student's initials are written on the masking tape. Each athlete will have three tries to throw the Frisbee as far as he or she can. When all Frisbees have been thrown, the judges will measure the longest distance for each athlete. The three athletes with the longest throws will receive the gold, silver, and bronze medals.

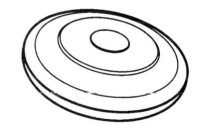

Help Needed: Ideally, this event needs at least two volunteers. These two volunteers will serve as judges and measure the distance that athletes were able to throw the Frisbees. Judges will record the distances on the event record sheet.

Athletic Olympic Event Descriptions *(cont.)*

Individual Events *(cont.)*

✢ Standing Long Jump

Materials Needed: masking tape to mark the jumping point, measuring tape or meter stick, event record sheet (page 81), pencil

Directions: Each athlete will have three tries to jump from a marked starting line. There will be no running prior to the jumping. The athlete must stand on the designated line and jump. The athlete can use his or her arms to propel himself/herself forward. The judges will then measure the jumps with a measuring tape or stick. Keep a record of the jumps for each athlete. The three athletes with the farthest jumps will be awarded the gold, silver, or bronze medals. If an athlete falls backwards or steps over the line, the attempt is disqualified.

Help Needed: A minimum of two volunteers are needed to serve as judges. One judge will stand at the starting line holding one end of the measuring tape. while the other judge measures the other end of the jump. One of the judges will need to record the jumps on the record sheet.

✢ High Jump

Materials Needed: wall (preferably an outdoor wall that can be written on with chalk), chalk, measuring tape, event record sheet (page 81), pencil

Directions: Each athlete will stand next to a wall with a piece of chalk in his or her hand. The athlete then jumps up as high as possible, and marks the wall with the chalk. Each athlete will have three tries at jumping. The judge will measure the highest jump for each athlete. The three athletes with the highest jumps will be awarded the gold, silver, or bronze medals.

Help Needed: This event needs a minimum of one volunteer. This volunteer will serve as a judge to make sure athletes are jumping correctly and to measure the height of each jump.

✢ Shuttle Run

Materials Needed: masking tape to mark start/finish line and turn-around line, block or other small item, stopwatch, event record sheet, pencil

Directions: The athlete will start at the start line. The block is placed at the turn-around line. At the word go, the athlete will run to the turn-around line, pick up the block, and race back across the finish line. The athlete must cross the turn-around line before returning. If the block is dropped, the run is disqualified. The athlete has two runs. The athlete with the fastest run will win the gold.

Help Needed: This race needs two volunteers. These volunteers serve as judges. These judges will tell the athletes when to go and the judges will time the runners. Only the fastest times are recorded.

Athletic Olympic Event Descriptions *(cont.)*

Team Events

⁜ 4 x 50-meter Relay

(For younger students, you may choose to do shorter distance or do practice runs to prepare your students.)

Materials Needed: masking tape to mark the start/finish points for each runner, five batons (one for each team), measuring tape to measure out 50-meter segments on the track or field, whistle, stopwatches (one for each team), event record sheet (page 81)

Directions: This race is run by four people. It is a relay race. Each runner is spaced 50-meters apart. Each runner will run 50 meters and pass the baton on to the next runner. The next runner cannot go until he or she has the baton. This race should include both boys and girls. Each team will select four runners to race in the relay, and one (or more) team member to cheer for the team.

Help Needed: The relay race will need volunteers to help at the starting and finish lines and one at each passing of the baton. The volunteers at the starting line will get the first runners ready to race and will blow the whistle when it is time for the race to begin. The volunteers spaced at the different baton exchange location will watch to ensure that the batons are passed correctly, that the runners do not leave without taking the baton, and that no batons are dropped. If the baton is dropped, the team is disqualified.

The volunteers at the finish line use the stopwatches to time each team. The times are recorded. A gold medal will go to each member of the winning team. The same goes for the silver and the bronze teams.

⁜ Soccer Game

Materials Needed: soccer balls, soccer nets, referees, whistle, tape, or chalk to make boundary lines, timers, paper, bowl

Directions: Create the boundaries for the playing field using chalk or tape. Set the soccer nets up at either end. Write the names of each team on a slip of paper. Put these slips of paper into a bowl. Draw two names out of the bowl. These two teams will be the first to play against each other. Review soccer rules with the teams. The timer will be set for 15 minutes. The two teams have 15 minutes to score as many goals as possible. Once the time is up, the score is recorded, and the next two teams play against each other. The team that was able to score the most points (regardless of which team they played) is the gold-medal team. The team with the next highest amount of points receives the silver, and the third-highest receives the bronze. Not all teams will play each other.

Help Needed: You will need volunteers to referee the soccer games and keep track of the goals that are scored. You can have more than one game going on at the same time if you have enough referees.

Athletic Olympic Event Student Sign-Up

You are allowed to sign up for one individual event. Only one student per team can compete in each individual event, unless you have permission from your teacher. Sign your name below, next to the event in which you will be competing.

Boys' 50-meter dash

1. _____
2. _____
3. _____
4. _____
5. _____

Girls' 50-meter dash

1. _____
2. _____
3. _____
4. _____
5. _____

Girls' Frisbee Throw

1. _____
2. _____
3. _____
4. _____
5. _____

Boys' Frisbee Throw

1. _____
2. _____
3. _____
4. _____
5. _____

Boys' Standing Long Jump

1. _____
2. _____
3. _____
4. _____
5. _____

Girls' Standing Long Jump

1. _____
2. _____
3. _____
4. _____
5. _____

Girls' High Jump

1. _____
2. _____
3. _____
4. _____
5. _____

Boys' High Jump

1. _____
2. _____
3. _____
4. _____
5. _____

Boys' Shuttle Run

1. _____
2. _____
3. _____
4. _____
5. _____

Girls' Shuttle Run

1. _____
2. _____
3. _____
4. _____
5. _____

Athletic Events Record Sheet

Use this page to keep track of the results of the Olympic events. Write the distance or place of each student competing. Then look at the results and write in the names of the medal winners.

Boys' 50-meter dash

Gold: _____

Silver: _____

Bronze: _____

4th Place:_____

5th Place:_____

Girls' 50-meter dash

Gold: _____

Silver: _____

Bronze: _____

4th Place:_____

5th Placc:_____

Girls' Frisbee Throw

Gold: _____

Silver: _____

Bronze: _____

4th Place:_____

5th Place:_____

Boys' Frisbee Throw

Gold: _____

Silver: _____

Bronze: _____

4th Place:_____

5th Place:_____

Boys' Standing Long Jump

Gold: _____

Silver: _____

Bronze: _____

4th Placc:_____

5th Place:_____

Girls' Standing Long Jump

Gold: _____

Silver: _____

Bronze: _____

4th Place:_____

5th Place:_____

Girls' High Jump

Gold: _____

Silver: _____

Bronze: _____

4th Place:_____

5th Place:_____

Boys' High Jump

Gold: _____

Silver: _____

Bronze: _____

4th Place:_____

5th Place:_____

Boys' Shuttle Run

Gold: _____

Silver: _____

Bronze: _____

4th Place:_____

5th Place:_____

Girls' Shuttle Run

Gold: _____

Silver: _____

Bronze: _____

4th Place:_____

5th Place:_____

Academic Olympic Event

Make copies of this page and have students read the rules and directions. Be sure to discuss any questions that may arise.

Object of the Academic Event

The academic Olympic event does not test physical skill, it tests mental skill. Each team will compete against other teams for the correct answer. Questions will be asked in order. If a team answers a question incorrectly, this question is given to the next team to answer. The team with the most points at the end of the game is declared the winner and receives the gold medal.

Setting Up the Game

Each team will select a speaker for their team. Only the team speaker can give the answer. Team members can consult with one another to answer the question, but only the speaker for the team can say the answer. Each team will sit at a table. Team points are recorded on the board for everyone to see. Teams will have 30 seconds to discuss the question with team members. When the 30 seconds are up, the speaker for the team must give the answer right away.

The questions that are asked during this academic Olympic event are about topics and information the students have studied throughout this unit. Some questions that are student-generated will be included with the other questions. The teacher or parent helper will be the judge. Students will need to understand that what the judge decides must stand and there will be no arguing. The game is over once a predetermined number of questions have been answered, or a designated amount of time (45 minutes to one hour) has taken place.

Game Preparation

Prior to the beginning of the game, students will work as a team to create three questions. These questions may or may not be asked during the course of the game, and there is on guarantee which team will end up answering these questions. These questions and their answers should be recorded below.

Question #1: _____

_____

Answer: _____

Question #2: _____

_____

Answer: _____

Question #3: _____

_____

Answer: _____

Academic Olympic Event Questions

The following questions, as well as the student-generated questions, should be used in the Academic Olympic Event Contest. You should read and preview all questions prior to the start of the game. Answers are listed in italics.

1. Who were the only people allowed to compete in the ancient Olympic Games? (*men and boys*)

2. What do the rings on the Olympic flag stand for? (*the continents that participate in the Olympic Games*)

3. What must a city have to host the Winter Games? (*snow*)

4. What is used to light the Olympic flame? (*the Olympic torch*)

5. What is the prize for second place at the Olympic Games? (*silver medal*)

6. Who weren't allowed to participate in the ancient Olympic Games? (*women and girls*)

7. In what year did the ancient Olympic Games begin? (*approximately 776 B.C.*)

8. In which country did the modern Olympic Games begin? (*Greece*)

9. What did winners in the ancient Olympic Games receive? (*olive wreaths*)

10. What is a chariot? (*a two-wheeled carriage pulled by four horses*)

11. Which Olympic Games has more events, summer or winter? (*summer*)

12. Who leads the athletes in reciting the Olympic Oath? (*usually one of the athletes from the host city*)

13. What country held the first Olympic Winter Games? (*France*)

14. What country has hosted the most Olympic Games? (*United States of America*)

15. What did the ancient judges wear? (*purple robes*)

16. What did the five rings stand for in ancient Greece? (*the number of years between the Olympics*)

17. What is one of the words in the Olympic motto in English? (*Swifter, Higher, Stronger*)

18. Who first entered the arena during the ancient Games? (*the judges*)

19. When is the Olympic flame lit? (*during the Opening Ceremonies*)

20. What does the third place winner receive? (*a bronze medal*)

Olympic Committees

Staging a class or school Olympic Games requires the help of all students. Assigning students to a committee allows all students to work together to bring about this exciting event. Assign different groups of students to work on a different committee than the teams that are used for the Olympics. This allows students to work with other students and gives fair representation for all of the teams on the committees. Listed below are the responsibilities for each committee. There are five committees. Ask parent volunteers to be the managers of each committee. Meet with all adult volunteers to explain assignments and how each of the committees will work.

Decorating and Advertising Committee

Materials Needed: white construction paper, markers, wooden dowels, crepe paper, and balloons (*optional*)

Directions: The responsibility for this committee is to advertise the Olympic Games around the school for classes that may want to come and watch. Posters listing the times, dates, and locations need to be made to promote the Olympic events.

Committee members will also need to make decorations to help create the Olympic spirit. Students can make Olympic flags that can be hung and placed in the area of the Olympic Games and of the Opening and Closing Ceremonies. You can also decorate the site for the Opening and Closing Ceremonies with crepe paper and balloons, if desired.

Documenting and Reporting Committee

Materials Needed: video camera, battery, cut cards (*optional*), paper, pencils

Directions: This committee is responsible for videotaping the Olympic activities. They will need to coordinate their schedules during the Olympic events so that they can all compete.

This committee has varying roles. One person will be the cameraperson. This person will, with the help of an adult, do the video recording (except when he/she is competing) of the Olympic Games. Another person will be the weather person. The weather person should use maps to show the viewing audience what to expect in the way of weather for the day of the Olympic Games. You will need two or three field reporters that are stationed around the Olympic Games. These reporters can plan interviews with all athletes, not just the winners. Field reporters will search for interesting stories about these young athletes and their families. Reporters can also report on the history of the events at this Olympic Games. Don't forget that the Opening and Closing Ceremonies should also be documented.

Olympic Committees *(cont.)*

Here are the instructions for the last three committees. Be sure to review these with each committee. Students need a clear understanding of what their assignment is.

Ceremony Committee

Materials Needed: CD player, musical recordings of the World Anthem and other marching/celebration music, camera, film, U.S. flag

Directions: This committee is responsible for the organization and preparations needed for the Opening and Closing Ceremonies. Students in this committee should read through the Opening and Closing Ceremonies plans on page 86.

Judging and Recording Committee

Materials Needed: stopwatches, measuring sticks, parent helpers, large construction paper, and markers

Directions: Under the direction of parent volunteers, this committee will be responsible for recording results and keeping score. If a student is competing, he or she will not be recording or judging.

Once the scores and times have been determined, and the recipients of gold, silver, and bronze are realized, this committee should create signs listing the results. These signs should be posted in a prominent place.

Teacher Note: Be sure to meet with parent volunteers prior to the day of the Olympic Games. You will want to review the rules and procedures for each event and to clarify how the times and distances should be counted and recorded. Be sure to answer all questions parent volunteers may have prior to the day of the events. You will be too busy that day to try and clarify the rules and guidelines.

Celebration and Awards Committee

Materials Needed: copies of page 92 (Olympic Medals), copies of page 93 (Olympic Certificates), copies of page 91 (Olive-Leaf Headband), 3-hole punch, construction paper (yellow, gray, and brown), colored markers, scissors, ribbon, cardboard (*optional*)

Directions: Using the copies of the pages mentioned in the materials section, students will design what the gold, silver, and bronze medals will look like. Once the design has been created, these can be copied on colored construction paper (yellow, gray, and light brown). These can be mounted on cardboard, if desired.

Students on this committee should make copies of the participation certificates and write student names on these. The olive-leaf headbands are optional and can be created to make headbands for medal winners.

Opening Ceremonies

Parade of Athletes

Students will parade around the school or around the playground. Students will walk as a team and each team will be wearing the team color previously assigned. Select one student to lead the parade. This student will carry the U.S. flag. The first person at the head of each team will carry the official team flag. The other team members can carry Olympic torches or smaller team flags. The teams will parade into the classroom or designated spot for the Opening Ceremonies. Have students set their flags on display.

Background Music

As students participate in the Olympic parade, you can play the Olympic theme song: *World Anthems,* performed by Donald Fraser and the English Chamber Orchestra. Audio CD (one disc). BMG/RCA Victor, 6321, 1998. AISN: B000007QCU. You can play other patriotic songs or marching songs to help the mood.

Photo Opportunity

With team members dressed in the five Olympic colors, you can arrange students in the shape of the Olympic rings and take a picture. Stand on chairs so you can get a top view of the "Olympic Rings."

Olympic Oath

When students reach the site of the Games, lead the students in reciting the Olympic Oath, pausing at each comma so that they can repeat after you:

> *In the name of all competitors, I promise that we shall take part in these Olympic Games, respecting and abiding by the rules that govern them, in the true spirit of sportsmanship, for the glory of the sport, and the honor of our teams.*

Closing/Awards Ceremonies

Parade of Athletes

Athletes march back to the Ceremony location. Students do not walk in as teams, but they walk in with other teams and classmates. Again, you can play background music, perhaps something with an upbeat rhythm to celebrate.

Awarding of Medals

You can present the awards and medals to the students or you can invite a guest, such as the principal, a P.E. teacher, or a special guest. The Awards Committee makes medals ahead of time. (See page 92 for instructions.) You can also present participatory certificates (see page 93) to students who participated but did not win a medal; or you can choose to give all students a participatory certificate.

Team Cheer

Have each team call out their team cheer and have the class clap for the effort of each team. Refreshments can be served after the awards and the parade of athletes.

Reporting the News

Create a class newspaper documenting the events of the Olympic Games. Imagine that you have been assigned to be a reporter of the events taking place. Use the newspaper format below for the paper. Younger students can draw pictures instead of writing articles.

OLYMPIC DAILY NEWS

In the News...

Today's Latest Information

Classified Advertisements

Olympic News

Olympic Cartoons

Fine-Arts Festival

The early members of the Olympic Games Committee did not want the Olympic Games to be merely a sports competition. From 1912 through 1948, medals were also awarded for excellence in the fine arts. The rules stated that projects were to be entered in the fields of architecture, sculpture, painting, music, and literature. The works were to be inspired by sports.

Directions: Decide as a class on the type of medium that your class will use to create a project to display at the Fine-Arts Festival. Some of the mediums to consider are literature, writing, paint, clay, or colored pencils. For younger students, you will need to discuss and walk through each step together as a class. With older students, you can have students fill out the form below to guide their project.

Fine-Arts Project

Name: _____

The project I am doing is_____

_____

The materials I will need are _____

_____

This is what I will do for my project: _____

_____

_____

Teacher Approval: _____

School Plan vs. Classroom Plan

You can alter the plans for the class Olympic Games to accommodate a school-wide or grade-level Olympic Games. Here are some suggestions or alterations you can use to make the adjustment:

Olympic Teams

With a larger group of athletes involved, you can assign classes a country to represent at the school-wide Olympic Games. Assign each country/team the responsibility to create a country flag to carry and post at the Opening Ceremonies. You can have each grade level wear an assigned color of the Olympic Rings so that you can still take a picture of the Olympic Rings formation. (You will probably have to be standing on something taller than a chair to take this picture.)

Opening Ceremonies

The opening ceremonies can be easily adapted to include a larger group. Designate a parade route for all the classes willing to participate. Classes/countries will march together following their country flag. All the athletes can take the Olympic Oath, with the principal leading the pledge.

With a larger group participating, the opening ceremonies can take on a more spectacular feel. Encourage students who are interested to create dances, songs, poetry, and other performances. These can be shared as part of the Opening Ceremonies. You can invite the school band, chorus/choir, and any other cultural clubs to perform at the ceremonies, as well.

Olympic Athletic Events

With more athletes competing, you will need more time to run the athletic events. You can assign a different day for each level to compete. For example, kindergarten students compete on Monday, first grade on Tuesday, second grade on Wednesday, and so forth until all grade levels have had a chance to compete. You will need to award medals for each grade level, as the skills and abilities will be different based on ages.

1. **Individual Events**—Students will still be able to compete in Olympic events, but there will need to be qualifying races. Students will sign up for one event in which they would like to compete. On the day of the Olympic Games, students will be assigned a heat in which to race. The top one or two finishers from each race will be in the final race. (You can adjust the number of qualifying finishers based on the number of students racing.)

2. **Team Events**—Team events can take place as instructed in the class Olympic Games. The only difference will be the number of team events. You can make a sign-up sheet listing a variety of team events—for example volleyball, basketball, kickball, soccer, tug-of-war, etc. Each class will decide which team event they will participate in. Students can rotate throughout the game to allow as many students as possible a chance to play. Each class will be allowed to sign up for only one team event. They will be competing against another class, and that will be the only team event in which these two teams/classes will compete.

School Plan vs. Classroom Plan *(cont.)*

Olympic Academic Event

A team from each class will represent their class/country at the Academic Olympic event. You should follow the same directions as outlined on page 82 for the Academic Olympic Event.

Fine-Arts Festival

Select a large room such as the cafeteria or gym to display all of the student art projects. These should be completed prior to the Olympic Games and set up before the competition begins. This would be a nice place to hold the Opening and Closing Ceremonies.

Parent Volunteers and Helpers

In order for a school-wide or grade-level Olympic Games to take place, you will need many parents. Teachers can meet and determine the responsibilities each class and grade level will have. These teachers can meet individually with their group of parents to explain the role and help needed from parents.

Materials: Stopwatches, timers, bases, balls, and all types of materials will be needed for these Olympic Games. Coordinate materials with other teachers and see if the P.E. teacher can give a hand.

Olympic Committees

Again, there is a lot of work for students to become involved in to stage these Olympic Games. The responsibilities for each committee remain the same. See pages 84–85 for these instructions. You may choose to assign classes to be in charge of specific committees. In order to host a school-wide Olympic Games, you may wish to add the following committees:

1. **Information Committee**—This committee would be responsible for providing information on the day of the Olympic Games. This committee can create maps of the Olympic events and direct students where they need to be.

2. **Newspaper Committee**—This committee could actually take pictures and write newspaper articles about the sights and sounds of the Olympic Games. This newspaper could be published and distributed school-wide a few days after the events. This keepsake could be autographed by gold-medal winners.

3. **Refreshment Committee**—This committee could be responsible for providing ice water and cups to all the athletes competing. If it is a hot day, this committee will be especially important so students do not need to stand in line at the drinking fountain. Be sure to have a trash receptacle handy to dispose of all the paper cups.

Closing Ceremonies

At the Closing Ceremonies, student athletes should walk in together. Medals and certificates should be awarded by the principal, a teacher, or another special guest. Parents can be invited to attend the ceremony. The school song could be played in conclusion, and the school mascot should be invited to attend and help celebrate!

Olive-Leaf Headbands

Color each of the leaves green. Cut out the leaves and staple to a green construction paper headband to create an olive-leaf headband.

Olympic Medals

Create designs for each of the medals below. Color one medal gold, one silver, and one bronze. Punch out the holes on each side of the tabs. Attach yarn or ribbon to create necklaces.

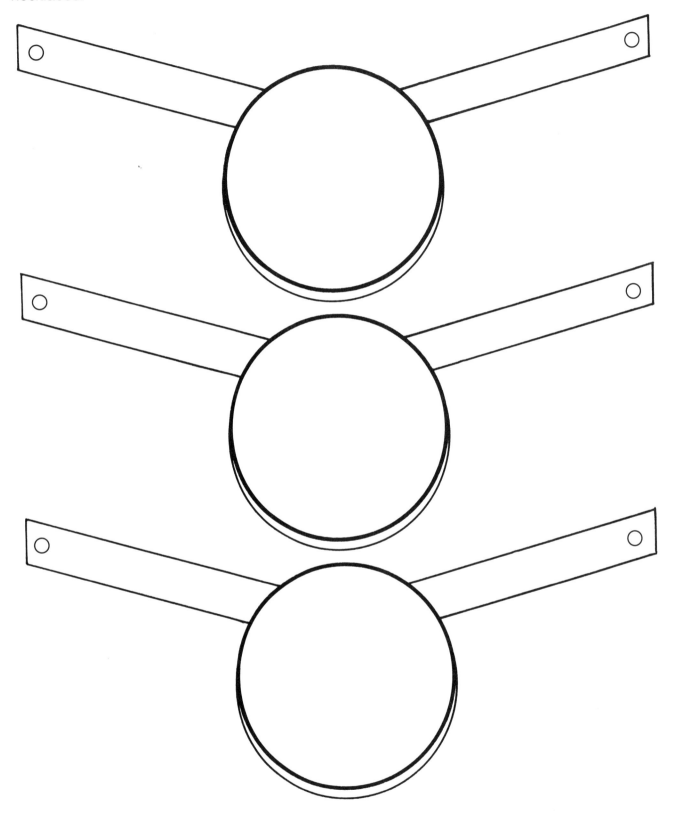

Olympic Certificate

Proud Participant

in the

Mini-Olympic

Games

Student's Name

Teacher/Coach

Date

Olympic Journal Entry

Did you have fun at the Olympic Games? Record your feelings below. Draw a picture below of you competing in the Olympic Games.

_____

_____

_____

_____

_____

_____

_____

Answer Key

Page 13—Olympic Trivia
1. only men and boys
2. approx. 776 B.C.
3. olive-leaf crowns
4. purple robes
5. 1900
6. athletes from Greece
7. peace
8. the Olympic torch
9. silver medal
10. two years
11. Athens, Greece
12. the five competing continents
13. summer
14. France
15. Swifter, Higher, Stronger
16. gold medal

Page 23—Map of Ancient Greece
1. Mt. Olympus
2. Delphi
3. Marathon
4. Athens
5. Sparta
6. Olympia
7. Corinth

Page 30—Olympic Medals and Rewards
1. United States
2. Italy
3. seven
4. Australia, Germany, China
5. Answers will vary.

Page 44—The Olympic Games and the World
1. Spain
2. Europe
3. Italy
4. Argentina
5. Belgium
6. Netherlands
7. traditions

Page 47—What Does it Say?
1. 0
2. 8
3. 1
4. 4
5. 3
6. 5
7. 7
8. 2
9. 1
10. 10
11. 4
12. 8
13. 9
14. 5
15. 6
16. 1
17. 2
18. 1
19. 3
20. 2

Motto: Swifter, Higher, Stronger

Page 63—It's All in a Word
1. aim
2. softball
3. taekwando
4. swimming
5. athletics
6. target

Bibliography

Anderson, Dave. *The Story of the Olympics.* HarperCollins Juvenile Books, 2000.

Bauer, Larry. *Easy Olympic Sports Readers.* Teacher Created Materials, 1988.

Brimmer, Larry Dane. *Bobsledding & the Luge.* School & Library Binding, 1997.

————. *Winter Olympics.* School & Library Binding, 1997. (Grades K–3)

Carlson, Lewis H. and John J. Fogarty. *Tales of Gold.* Contemporary Books, 1987.

Crowler, Robert. *Robert Crowler's Pop-Up Olympics: Amazing Facts and Record Breakers.* Candlewick Press, 1996.

Coote, James. *A Picture History of the Olympics.* Macmillan, 1972.

Davida. Kristy. *Coubertin's Olympics: How the Games Began.* Leiner Publications Co., 1995.

Ditchfield, Christin. *Cycling.* Children's Press, 2000. (Grades K–3)

————. *Gymnastics.* Children's Press, 2000. (Grades K–3)

————. *Kayaking, Canoeing, and Yachting.* Children's Press, 2000.

————. *Swimming and Diving.* Children's Press, 2000. (Grades K–3)

————. *Wrestling.* Children's Press, 2000. (Grades K–3)

Hennessy, B.G. *Olympics!* Viking Penguin Books, 1996.

Holzschuler, Cynthia. *United States Olympic Committee's Curriculum Guide to the Olympic Games: The Dream.* Griffin Publishing Group/Teacher Created Materials, Inc., 2000.

Knotts, Bob. *Equestrian Events.* Children's Press, 2000. (Grades K–3)

————. *Martial Arts.* Children's Press, 2000. (Grades K–3)

————. *The Summer Olympics.* Children's Press, 2000. (Grades K–3)

————. *Track & Field.* Children's Press, 2000. (Grades K–3)

————. *Weight Lifting.* Children's Press, 2000. (Grades K–3)

Ledeboer, Suzanne. *Olympism: A Basic Guide to the History, Ideals, and Sports of the Olympic Movement.* Griffin Publishing Group, 2001.

Osbourne, Mary Pope. *Hour of the Olympics.* Random House, 1998.

Oxlade, Chris, and David Ballheimer. *Eyewitness: Olympics.* Dorling Kindersley Publishing, Inc., 2000.

Web Sites

- *www.education-world.com/a_sites/sites047.shtml*
  This is Education World's site for teaching about the Olympic Games. It offers links to sites containing free lesson plans.

- *www.usoc.org*
  This is the official Web site of the United States Olympic Committee (USOC).

- *www.timeforkids.com*
  This site offers the latest information on recent or upcoming Olympic events.

- *www.sikids.com*
  This Sports Illustrated site is ranked one of the top kids' sites in Yahoo! Internet Life's 100 Best Sites of 2000.

- *www.olympics.org*
  Offers daily news updates on the Olympic Games, medal totals, and individual athletes.